Edith Wharton

A Woman in Her Time

Edith Wharton

A Woman in Her Time

LOUIS
AUCHINCLOSS

A Studio Book • The Viking Press • New York

For my sister-in-law, Audrey Auchincloss

ACKNOWLEDGMENTS

My collection of the letters of Edith Wharton has been made up entirely through the generosity of the following friends, whose relatives (or in some cases who themselves) were the recipients of the letters: Dagmar W. Sargent, Julia M. Welldon, Audrey M. Auchincloss, Walter Maynard, Katharine H. Osborn, Frederic R. King, Shiela B. Lawrence, Frederica R. Landon, Laura C. White, Ellis Russell (as executor of the will of Mildred B. Bliss), the late Pauline Robinson, and the late Margaret T. Chanler.

I am deeply indebted to Julia Newbold Cross for her gift of the copy of the 1878 *Verses* which belonged to her aunt, Edith Newbold, and which was inscribed by Edith Newbold Jones to Edith Newbold.

In the selection of pictures I am happy to acknowledge the invaluable assistance of the Beinecke Rare Book Library at Yale and of Frederic R. King.

For suggestions and ideas with respect to the preparation of the text, I owe much to illuminating conversations with Leon Edel and R. W. B. Lewis.

CONTENTS

1

BROWNSTONE CHILDHOOD

Somebody once observed that Edith Wharton and Theodore Roosevelt, despite a common background of moneyed Manhattan, were both "self-made men." It is true. They were born, only three years and three blocks apart, into the same tight, privileged world of "Old New York," but they rebelled against the complacency of a point of view that found politics too dirty for gentlemen and letters too inky for ladies. Edith Wharton was to describe the enervating effect of this gentle, mocking world on Newland Archer, the hero of *The Age of Innocence*. We see how relentlessly it closes in on him, and how, toward the end of a temperate life of minor accomplishments, he has little to show but the friendship of "one great man." This great man is Theodore Roosevelt who, like Archer's creator, had freed himself from the miasma of that early innocence.

Amy Lowell, though a Bostonian, echoed the same theme when she said that her greatest handicap was to have been born into a class which was commonly assumed to be incapable of artistic creativity. How, then, do we explain Henry James? Did he not grow up, at least in part, in Edith Wharton's New York? Is not *Washington Square* concerned with the same society as *The Age of Innocence?* Yet James, surely, had the

Childe Hassam,
New York win-
ter street scene.

ideal upbringing for a writer. His father, his brother, his sister, all wrote. He met Emerson and Thackeray as a boy, Turgenev and Flaubert as a young man. He called on George Eliot and heard Tennyson read. Wherein lay the difference?

It lay in the difference between two intersecting circles of the same small *haute bourgeoisie*. It is entirely possible that Henry James, Sr., may have met Edith Wharton's father, George Frederic Jones, or even that they had friends in common. From the standpoint of a European they would have appeared to belong to precisely the same world. But seen from Washington Square, they were quite distinct. The Jameses were more like the English Arnolds or Darwins, a deeply congenial family of inherited means and large ideas whose generations were united by a love of the arts and sciences. Young Henry was encouraged from the beginning to become a writer. Not so Edith Jones. In the more fashionable group to which her parents belonged, a nodding acquaintance with the arts was all that was considered necessary. Even after she had become a published author, her literary activities were a subject of mild embarrassment to many of her family circle. In Boston (her husband's city), as she later wrote, she was considered too fashionable to be intelligent, and in New York too intelligent to be fashionable.

One has only to read Proust to see how many varying cliques can exist about the apex of a single social pyramid. Both Jameses and Joneses went to Newport, but this brought them no closer together. Maud Howe Elliott, a daughter of Newport's literary patroness, Julia Ward Howe, and one of the Jameses' circle, wrote of Edith ("Pussy") Jones: "Our acquaintance was slight, she belonging to the ultra-fashionable crowd, and I in quite another group. Though the intellectuals and the fashionables met, they never quite fused. She was slender, graceful and icy cold, with an exceedingly aristocratic bearing." Even after her marriage Edith was not for a long time to break into any group that contained artists or literary persons. As her friend Mrs. Winthrop Chanler put it: "The Four Hundred would have fled in a body from a poet, a painter, a musician or a clever Frenchman."

No apology need be offered for dwelling at some length on the social background of Edith Wharton's early years. It

Edith in her teens.

has been said that childhood is a novelist's whole capital, and this seems particularly true in her case. She was never able altogether to escape the New York and Newport of her youth. It

Interior of the Jones house on West 23rd Street. "Drawing rooms are always tidy."

was one of those love-hate relationships that pursue their victims to the end. The Atlantic Ocean came to seem to her a belt which not only divided the great international capitals from a provincial, even a parochial New York, but which separated the cultural centers of the Old World from the prosaic and deadly materialism of her American beginnings. In London and Paris she found the cultivated, sympathetic souls whom she had not found at home, and in time she gave up even visiting her native shores and went so far in signalizing her renunciation as to instruct her sister-in-law, Mrs. Cadwalader Jones, that it was no longer necessary to cable but merely to write news of the deaths of old New York friends and acquaintances. Yet

with the breakup of Europe of the *belle époque* in the First World War her glances westward became imbued with nostalgia. All her life she craved order and admired discipline, and she came to suspect that these values had existed more importantly in the city of her childhood than she had originally thought. There was always a half-mocking, half-respectful note in her evocations of old Manhattan customs. A young American woman who had gone to the theater in Paris with a gentleman friend was startled to hear Mrs. Wharton's sharp carrying voice in a row behind her: "I didn't know that Julia Hoyt was engaged!" In *her* day such would have been the only polite conclusion to be drawn. It probably amused her to startle young people with old constructions of their conduct. But if she smiled at the naïve formalities of the *ancien régime*, she may have a bit condescendingly pitied those who did not even know what they were.

She was born on West 23rd Street in New York in 1862, the daughter of George Frederic and Lucretia Rhinelander Jones, and we pause again here. *Was* she the daughter of

Edith's father, George Frederic Jones.

George Frederic Jones? An old legend exists, without any foundation of fact that I have been able to discover, that she was the daughter of Lucretia Jones and the young English tutor of her two older sons, Frederic and Harry. The tutor is reputed to have gone West and been killed by Indians. Wayne Andrews finds support for the legend in Edith's use of illegitimacy in some of her plots, but surely the unsuspecting bastard

16

("Don't hit him! He's your father!") was a favorite device of her generation of writers. I suggest that the legend sprang rather from the inability of New York society to believe that it could have produced a female author of such standing. Edith was much younger than the other Jones children, was she not? And the only intellectual of her family? And the tutor, was he not clever? Q. E. D.! Such theorizing, one may note in passing, is

Edith's mother, Lucretia Rhinelander Jones.

just the opposite of that which insists on making Shakespeare a peer. I drop the subject with only two observations. First, Edith Wharton knew of the legend herself and shrugged it away. Mrs. Chanler told me that when they were motoring together in England, Edith remarked with a little smile as they passed through a small village: "This is where my 'father' came from." Second, although in her memoirs she had considerably more to say of her mother's family than of the Joneses, she nevertheless put in, as illustrations, two full-page portraits of her father and of her paternal grandfather, Edward Renshaw Jones. The latter looks just like her.

The Joneses were well-off but not rich. They *had* been rich, before the standard had been hopelessly elevated by the Astors, to whom, through the Schermerhorns, they were closely related. George Templeton Strong, describing a gallery filled with the "magnates of what's called society," wrote that it included "all the Astors and lots of Joneses." Edith's parents, like many of their group, derived a comfortable income from municipal real estate, which enabled them, until the inflation that followed the Civil War, to keep up a brownstone in Manhattan, a much larger place (Pencraig) in Newport, and to travel in Europe when they wished. The Rhinelanders, Edith's mother's family, were not rich, but they were closely related to plenty of people who were, including the "rich" Rhinelanders. The Joneses were intermarried with Pendletons,

OPPOSITE: Pencraig, the Jones house in Newport, Rhode Island. ABOVE: Interior of Pencraig. Two portraits of Edith can be seen to the left.

Gallatins, and Schermerhorns; the Rhinelanders with Stevenses, Ledyards, and Newbolds. It was a closed world where nobody engaged in retail trade, where nobody, for that matter, engaged in very much of anything. The great Vanderbilt clan, which was to change the faces of Fifth Avenue and Newport, was still in the wings. The only titans in society were the Astors and August Belmont, who dazzled Manhattan with his opulence and who was to appear as Julius Beaufort in *The Age of Innocence*. He was setting the style of the future, but this was not generally realized. Looking back over her family tree, Edith clung to the

Dancing on the grass at the meeting of the Coaching Club.

Meeting of the Coaching
Club in Newport, 1893.

image of her great-grandfather, Ebenezer Stevens, a Revolutionary patriot and merchant. His energy seemed to have been lost.

OPPOSITE: Edith's grandfather, Edward Renshaw Jones, whose striking resemblance helps discount idle legends of illegitimacy. ABOVE: The earliest known likeness of Edith.

One need not attempt to picture the daily life of Edith's parents when she has done so herself:

> The child of the well-to-do, hedged in by nurses and governesses, seldom knows much of its parents' activities. I have only the vaguest recollection of the way in which my father and mother spent their days. I know that my father was a director on the principal charitable boards of New York—the Blind Asylum and the Bloomingdale Insane Asylum among others; and that during Lent a ladies' "sewing class" met at our house to work with my mother for the poor. I also recall frequent drives with my mother, when the usual afternoon round of card-leaving was followed by a walk in the Central Park, and a hunt for violets

ABOVE LEFT: Edith at age of eight. ABOVE RIGHT: Edith's oldest brother, Frederic Rhinelander Jones, whose divorced wife, Mary Cadwalader Jones, remained Edith's lifelong friend and literary agent. OPPOSITE: Edith's brother Harry Jones, whose later life and marriage aroused her disapproval.

and hepaticas in the secluded dells of the Ramble. In the evenings my parents went occasionally to the theatre, but never, as far as I remember, to a concert, or any kind of musical performance, until the Opera, then only sporadic, became an established entertainment, to which one went (as in eighteenth-century Italy) chiefly if not solely for the pleasure of conversing with one's friends. Their most frequent distraction was dining out or dinner giving. Sometimes the dinners were stately and ceremonious (with engraved invitations issued three weeks in advance, soups, "thick" and "clear," and a Roman punch half way through the *menu*), but more often they were intimate and sociable, though always the occasion of much excellent food and old wine being admirably served, and discussed with suitable gravity.

It is important to remember the solitude of this "child of the well-to-do." Edith's two brothers were so much older as to put her in the position, practically speaking, of an only child. One sees in the portrait of her a girl of a very composed, an almost prim demeanor: the little lady who is very aware that she is a little lady. This was not brushed off, either, by any

24

rough-and-tumble with her contemporaries. Education was not
by school but by governesses. We receive a picture of how the
Joneses' drawing room must have appeared to the young Edith
in a letter that she wrote, decades later, to her sister-in-law
about the staging of Zoë Akins' dramatization of *The Age of
Innocence*. This dramatization, incidentally, was never pro-

Fifth Avenue and 61st Street, looking south in 1899, showing the Elbridge
Gerry house, designed by Richard Morris Hunt.

duced, though a later one, by Margaret Ayer Barnes, enjoyed some success on Broadway with Katharine Cornell as its star.

I am very anxious about the staging and dressing. I could do every stick of furniture and every rag of clothing myself, for every detail of that far-off scene was indelibly stamped on my infant brain. I am so much afraid that the young actors will be "summit collar" athletes, with stern faces and shaven lips, instead of gentlemen. Of course they ought all to have moustaches—and not toothbrush ones, but curved and slightly twisted at the ends. They should wear dark gray frock coats and tall hats, and always a button-hole—violets by day, a gardenia in evening dress. White waistcoats with their evening clothes and pumps, I *think*. But you will remember all this as well as I do. As for their *facerie* and their language, since you say that Miss Akins knows European society, please tell her that a New York drawing room of my childhood was far more like a London one, a du Maurier one, of old-fashioned gentlefolk, than anything that modern New York can give her. Above all, beg her to avoid slang and Americanisms, and tell her that English was then the language spoken by American ladies and gentlemen, since she is too young, I am sure, to have known those happy days herself. Few people nowadays know that many of the young men of our day (in N. Y.) were educated in English universities, and that English tutors and governesses were frequent, and that no girl went to a school, and that older women didn't wear pince-nez and white false-fronts. If she does not know this, and does not equally keep away from that grotesque stage invention of "Southern chivalry," she will never get the right atmosphere.

It is not easy to reconstruct Edith's relationships with her parents, except from what she does *not* say about them, in her memoirs. She speaks with considerable affection of her father,

27

but only in the passage about his premature and distressing death, and the terms which she uses in writing of her mother are all associated with coldness, formality, and appearance. One searches in vain in her novels for daughters who owe much to their mothers, although there are several examples of strong mother-son bonds. Lucretia Jones seems to be remembered chiefly for her style. She dressed well and spoke well; she obviously lived up to the standards of her world. There is the famous anecdote of Edith, at eleven, showing her mother the manuscript of a "novel" which began with a Mrs. Tomkins apologizing to a visitor for not having tidied up the drawing room. The work was returned with this icy comment which froze the child's creative frenzy: "Drawing rooms are always tidy." Yet such mothers are precisely those who gain the greatest hold on lonely daughters. I wonder, in seeking the answer of why Edith was so long in spreading her wings, if one need look much further than Lucretia Jones. She was probably just kind enough, just attractive enough, just wise enough, to make any act of rebellion seem to a child an act of bad taste.

Edith's isolation must have been intensified by the long trips that the Joneses took, in the interests of economy, to Europe. The depreciation of the currency in the late 1860s had so reduced their income that for a period of six years they lived largely in France and Italy. New Yorkers in that era did not cultivate European friendships; they were afraid of being snubbed by aristocrats who might not appreciate their high rung in the brownstone hierarchy of their native city. It was a life of hotels and watering places, of seeing only fellow Americans and their servants, but there were compensations for the sensitive child in driving out to the Roman Campagna and wandering among the tombs of the Appian Way, or in collecting fragments of porphyry and lapis lazuli on the slopes of the Palatine, or in such a Parisian sight as the Empress Eugénie in her *daumont*, with the little Prince Imperial at her side and a glittering escort of officers. Edith was to call the economic depression that had necessitated these trips a "happy misfortune" because it gave her, for the rest of her life, a background of beauty and old-established order. But I cannot but wonder if Edith, from first to last, did not have more of Europe than she strictly needed as a novelist.

It seems to me that she touches more closely on her real literary debt when she praises her family's use of English. The three elements of her education that she lists in her memoirs are (1) the modern languages, (2) good manners, and (3) "a reverence for the English language as spoken according to the best usage." Edith's parents, "who were far from intellectual, who read little and studied not at all," nevertheless spoke their mother tongue with scrupulous perfection and insisted that she do the same. "Where did you pick *that* up?" was Lucretia Jones's dry query to any bit of modern slang that crept into her daughter's conversation.

> We spoke naturally, instinctively good English, but my parents always wanted it to be better, more flexible and idiomatic. This excessive respect for the language never led to priggishness, or precluded the enjoyment of racy innovations. Long words were always smiled away as pedantic, and any really expressive slang was welcomed with amusement—but used as slang, as it were between quotation marks, and not carelessly admitted into our speech.

I cannot help but be of two opinions about this. Certainly Edith was right to acknowledge the debt which her own strong, cohesive, elastic style owed to her mother's training. But there may have been an occasional vividness sacrificed to propriety; an easy capaciousness, even whimsicality, lost to good breeding. Theodore Dreiser and Sinclair Lewis triumphed over faults of style. In one field at least Edith was to find the rules of good

Fifth Avenue, in 1895, looking east and south from the first Plaza Hotel. To the right is the "Marble Row," a group of houses built by Edith's cousin Mary Mason Jones, who figured as Mrs. Mingott in *The Age of Innocence*.

taste fatal: in poetry. Her poems never convey any of the emotion of her prose. They are exercises, correct but dead.

Just as important as the emphasis on language was the free use that she had and made of her father's library. Her family, with perfect logic, carried their prohibition of bad English over to the ephemeral rubbish of contemporary literature, so there was nothing to distract Edith from the classics on the paternal shelves. It was obvious, she tells us, though I am not sure how quickly we agree, that a little girl "to whom the Old Testament, the Apocalypse and the Elizabethan dramatists were open could not long pine for Whyte Melville or even Rhoda Broughton." In the sternly impressive list of her early reading, with its heavy emphasis on history and poetry, the only American names are Prescott, Parkman, Longfellow, and Irving. The other Melville, Herman, "a cousin of the Van Rensselaers, and qualified by birth to figure in the best society," she never, as a girl, even heard mentioned. Culture and education to the Joneses and to their group still meant Europe.

One small volume, happened upon in the house of a friend, seemed to burst into fiery bloom in Edith's hands. It was Swinburne:

> Forth, ballad, and take roses in both arms,
>   Even till the top rose touch thee in the throat
> Where the least thornprick harms;
>   And girdled in thy golden singing-coat,
> Come thou before my lady and say this:
>   Borgia, thy gold hair's colour burns in me,
> Thy mouth makes beat my blood in feverish rhymes;
>   Therefore so many as these roses be,
>   Kiss me so many times.

It is interesting that this stanza should have so abided in her memory for it represents exactly the goal to which her own versifying always reached and never remotely attained. It is literary, artificial, recklessly romantic, a style that produces mellifluous trash in hands other than Swinburne's. But for better or worse, Edith in her teens turned to poetry. Before then, one gathers, prose had been her chief concern. She describes her habit as a small girl of "making up," sitting with a book in her lap but writing nothing down, and, later, of scribbling stories and plays on brown wrapping paper, as no foolscap was supplied her. This latter touch would seem to throw the harshest light of all on the severity of Lucretia Jones.

ABOVE: Inscription in one of the rare surviving copies of *Verses*. "Edith Newbold. February 15th, 1879. E.N.J." Edith Newbold was Edith Newbold Jones's first cousin. OPPOSITE: Title page from *Verses*, 1878.

Her family, at any rate, must have changed their attitude about Edith's writing by her sixteenth year, for they presumably backed the private printing of her *Verses* in 1878 by C. E. Hammett in Newport. The legend that they bought up and destroyed the little paperbound volume is obviously absurd. Only some nine or ten copies survive, it is true, but the recipients could not be expected to realize that they had a "first" of a future novelist and to treasure it. My own copy is inscribed to "Edith Newbold," the author's first cousin. Obviously the poems must have been distributed among her family and friends

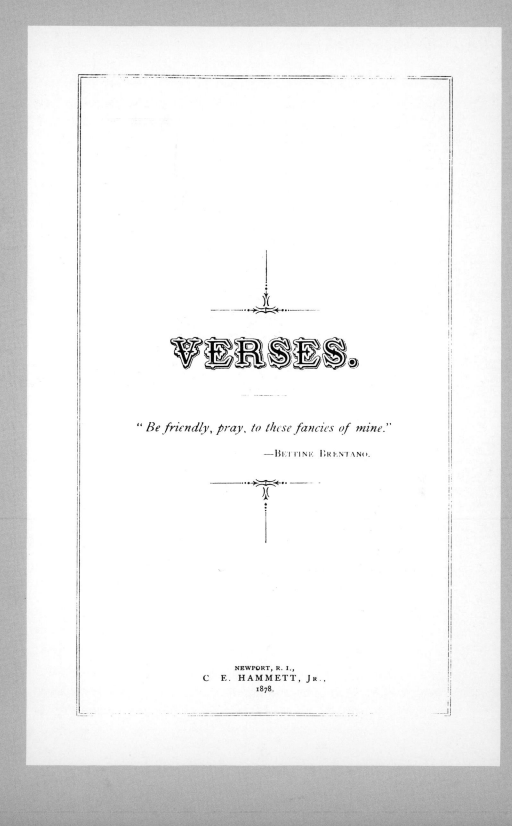

VERSES.

" Be friendly, pray, to these fancies of mine."

—Bettine Brentano.

NEWPORT, R. I.,
C. E. HAMMETT, Jr.,
1878.

"The Last Token."

A. D. 107.

(She speaks.)

One minute more of life! Enough to snatch
This flower to my bosom, and to catch
The parting glance and signal overhead
From one who sits and waits to see me dead.
One minute more! Enough to let him see
How straight the message fell from him to me,
And how, his talisman upon my breast,
I'll face the end as calmly as the rest.—
Th' impassive wall of faces seems to break
And shew one face aquiver for my sake * * *
How different death seems, with a hand that throws
Across the pathway of my doom a rose,
How brief and paltry life, compared to this
O'ertoppling moment of supremest bliss! * * *
Farewell! I feel the lions' hungry breath,
I meet your eyes * * * beloved, this is death.

1878.

OPPOSITE: Page from *Verses*. ABOVE: Charles E. Hammett, Jr., standing
before his bookstore and stationery shop, 202 Thames Street, Newport.

Miniature of Edith by Paillet, 1890.

with everybody's blessing. Besides, Maud Howe Elliott speaks of Newport's surprise when Pussy Jones, in her twenties, brought out a book of poetry. Her memory betrayed her about the age, but it is clearly *Verses* to which she is referring, for Edith did not publish her next volume of poetry until she was forty-seven. Nor does the complacent inscription in the author's own copy betray any sense of opposition:

> Who wrote these verses, she this volume owns.
> Her unpoetic name is Edith Jones.

The poems show a wide reading and a depth of literary feeling remarkable in a girl of sixteen, but very little inspiration. There are notes of Keats, Rossetti, Wordsworth, Swinburne, Browning. The dramatic monologues of the last named may have given the young poetess some sense of her own future vocation as a storyteller. In "The Last Token, A.D. 107" she excites a brief interest with a theatrical situation, however banal. A young woman in the Roman arena spies her lover in the watching crowd and catches the flower he tosses. We read her last thoughts:

> One minute more! Enough to let him see
> How straight the message fell from him to me,
> And how, his talisman upon my breast,
> I'll face the end as calmly as the rest.——
> Th' impassive wall of faces seems to break
> And shew one face aquiver for my sake * * *
> How different death seems, with a hand that throws
> Across the pathway of my doom a rose,
> How brief and paltry life, compared to this
> O'ertoppling moment of supremest bliss! * * *
> Farewell! I feel the lions' hungry breath,
> I meet your eyes * * * beloved, this is death.

We shall meet this rose-tossing spectator of his beloved's anguish again and again in the long gallery of Edith's fiction. The cool epicure of her dreams seems to have antedated all of his supposed counterparts.

2

MARRIAGE

Between *Verses* in 1878 and the publication of Edith's first story in *Scribner's* in 1891 lie thirteen years in which three published poems, one in the *Atlantic Monthly* and two in the *World*, are the only evidence of literary activity. Suppose one were to take the period from the ages of sixteen to twenty-nine out of the lives of the Brontë sisters, how much would be left? But Edith had a great many things to get through before she could settle down to even a part-time literary career. She had to "come out"; she had to help take care of a dying father; she had to become engaged, disengaged, and then, finally, engaged and married. All of these events occurred in the seven years between 1878 and 1885, in an era when any one of them would have been considered a full-time activity for a Miss Jones or Rhinelander.

I believe that in this period Edith may have been adapting herself, with resignation, perhaps even with cheerfulness, to the role that she expected to play in life: that of the fashionable society matron in New York and Newport. I doubt that she considered that she was giving up a literary career for this. The *Verses*, to which she never seems to have referred, must have soon struck her as an embarrassing reminder of the ebullience of youth. A young girl could not stay in her father's library

Edith against a photographer's backdrop.

forever, and when she emerged, where did she find herself but in the drawing room?

Maud Howe Elliott had found her elegant, icy cold. But stiffness is the classic armor of shy people. Years later Edith was to describe shyness as the "dread disease" which had "martyrized" her youth. It is also noteworthy that she had to contend with a distinct lack of beauty. Edith had a fine figure and good eyes, but her face was too long, her chin too determined. Her movements were jerky. In all her posed photographs she is grave, dignified, regal, but they bear little resemblance to the rather tense woman we see in snapshots. Edith was ultimately to make herself a very attractive woman, but she needed for this the self-confidence that comes with achievement. For a debutante in the 1880s, with the disadvantage of shyness and without the asset of beauty, social life must have seemed a fairly stiff task. I doubt that it was compatible with much serious literary work.

Edith may have suffered from a third disadvantage: the diminution of the Joneses' social position in a city that was being taken over by the new multimillionaires. It is hard to determine how much she noticed or minded such things, but after her father's death in 1882 she and the widowed Lucretia were alone in a city whose fantastic opulence and birthday-cake châteaux must have made their brownstone sobriety seem more shabby than genteel. It was all very well to sneer at the splendor of the Vanderbilts—and sneer the Joneses undoubtedly did—but fashions were changing, as Edith was vividly to record in *The House of Mirth*. The only way that old New York was going to save itself was by intermarrying with the new rich before all the latter's heiresses were grabbed up by less fastidious European peers. And it was happening already. A Livingston had married a Mills, as in an earlier day a Schermerhorn had married an Astor. By the 1890s the Vanderbilts would be well worth the Van Rensselaers.

Edith as a young matron, with the almost required tiara.

Something of this may have been behind Edith's engagement to Harry Stevens. Little is known of it except that it was brief. His mother, Mrs. Paran Stevens (not related to Edith's Revolutionary ancestor), was a rich and forceful woman of simple origins (a "cook" in the opinion of Lily Langtry, the English actress whom she snubbed) who had assailed and subdued Newport after the Civil War with the aid of a sister, Miss Fannie Reed, who sang at musicales. She married her

LEFT: Drawing room of Mrs. Paran Stevens' house at One East 57th Street, 1894. OPPOSITE: Mrs. Paran Stevens, in costume as Queen Elizabeth for the W. K. Vanderbilts' fancy-dress ball in 1883, the year her son was engaged to Edith.

daughter Minnie to an English Paget and was probably looking for something grander than a Jones for her son Harry when the latter fell in love with Edith. Harry was probably as weak in character as he was in health. He did not stand up to his mother, and he died young, in 1885, of an abdominal growth. The engagement seems to have been formed and dissolved in the summer of 1883.

I have a letter written from Newport by Edith's first cousin, Helen Rhinelander (then fifteen) to her brother Tom, which describes the event as follows:

> Is it not sad about Pussy's engagement being broken? I have only seen her once and then she did not appear particularly sad. It is evidently Mrs. S's fault, or rather she is the cause. We have not heard much about it, only Mrs. S behaved insultingly to Aunt Lu! Don't repeat this for the world. Aunt Lu told this to Mamma! I doubt Pussy and H have changed in their feeling for one another, but that Mrs. S is at the bottom of it all.

On the other hand W. H. Buckler, a friend of Edith's, recalling the incident in 1938, writes of the Patriarchs' Ball, in 1883, "at which my brother Julian White was Pussy Jones' partner and remembered vividly her nervousness at the staring of the N.Y. matrons whom she had just been shocking by breaking off her engagement with the son (Henry?) of Mrs. Stevens, considered a great matrimonial catch."

Both impressions could be true. Edith, even if maneuvered by Mrs. Stevens into breaking the engagement, might well have been criticized by matrons who did not know the full story. One wonders how deeply her feelings were involved. That she should have contemplated marrying for money alone seems inconsistent with her character as I see it, but she would have been an unusual young woman in the worldly society of the 1880s had she discounted Harry's fortune altogether. I doubt, anyway, that she long pined for a lover who was so easily manipulated by a brassy mother. There seems to be no trace of Harry that one can pick up in the record she has left, unless some aspects of his personality may have been repeated in the pleasant friend of her brother Fred, Edward Robbins Wharton, the Bostonian to whom she became engaged the following year.

Teddy at the time of his marriage.

Why? Commentators have asked the question through the decades. What did this brilliant and perceptive woman see in this ordinary and ultimately rather pathetic man? The trouble, of course, is that they see her marriage at the time of its breakup, when Edith was a famous author, surrounded by brilliant friends, and poor Teddy was an ailing neurasthenic striking out petulantly at a milieu that he neither liked nor understood. But that was not at all the way he must have appeared in 1885 to a young woman, five years "out," who was probably beginning to wonder (however unreasonably) if she was *ever* going to be married.

He was thirteen years older, but thirty-six in a man is nothing to a woman of twenty-three. He was associated with her older brother, which may (at least at that time) have auto-

Mrs George Frederic Jones requests the honour of your presence at the marriage of her daughter to Mr Edward R. Wharton at Trinity Chapel on Wednesday April twenty-ninth at twelve o'clock.

OPPOSITE: Edith's wedding invitation. ABOVE: Trinity Chapel on West 25th Street, where Edith and Teddy were married by the Reverend Morgan Dix on April 29, 1885.

matically put him in an admired category. He was handsome, easygoing, attractive, the sportsman and clubman who yet has an eye for a good picture, a palate for a good wine, a taste for lively people. Was Edith the first bluestocking (for despite all that Lucretia Jones and French dresses could do, there was always going to be *that* aspect of her) who has ever fallen in love with such a man? Could one not make the argument that

intellectual, literary women are actually prone to such experiences? Ellen Glasgow adored a man who shared none of her interests. George Eliot married one young enough to be her son. Mary McCarthy's first husband was an actor. Not all Elizabeth Barretts find Robert Brownings.

And then, too, Teddy Wharton offered such a pleasant solution to her problems. He was not rich—not in a Vanderbilt Newport, anyway—but he was well enough off to escape what she always regarded as the drudgery of American business life. For the first three years of their marriage they avoided New York and its increasingly oppressive social life altogether, dividing their time between Europe and Newport. Teddy was willing—at least in the early years—to let his wife take the lead. He followed in her wake to all the shrines of France and Italy, meticulous about timetables and accommodations, and always keeping a thousand-dollar bill in his wallet "in case Pussy wanted something." What normal young woman would not have preferred life with such a man to life with Lucretia Jones?

Of course, she was wrong. She and Teddy were deeply, fundamentally incompatible, and their superficial congeniality could not survive the glaring intimacy of marriage, particularly of a childless marriage. He loved the country life of sportsmen and thoughtless, easygoing people; she cared for books, for European sights, for scholars or, failing them, for dilettantes. He was proud of her brilliance, but pride is not patience. It must have been difficult for him to live with a woman who was so much his intellectual superior and who could never keep herself from showing it. Two decades later she was to note in

OPPOSITE: Pencraig Cottage, Newport, Rhode Island, where Edith and Teddy spent their first three married years. BELOW: Interior of Pencraig Cottage.

her secret journal (fragments of which were recently published) that on a train ride, when she had ventured to show Teddy a striking passage in R. H. Lock's study of heredity and variation, he had simply handed the book back with the query: "Does that sort of thing really amuse you?" One can understand the rebuff. It may have been a hot day and a long ride, and he may have been sick to death of his wife's relentless erudition. But Edith's answering cry (to her journal) is from the heart: "That is the answer to everything worthwhile! Oh, Gods of derision! And you've given me twenty years of it! *Je n'en peux plus.*"

Edith and Teddy in mourning.

Twenty years of it! Was there no happiness, even in the beginning? Alas, probably not. It could not have taken her long to see that nothing was going to change Teddy. From 1885 to the printing of her first story in 1891 is a period of less than six years, and the finished style of her early work suggests that she must have started writing some time before she started publishing: *i.e.*, not too long after her wedding. The same diary reveals that she could endure the "moral solitude" of life with Teddy only by creating a world of her imagination. This certainly substantiates Edmund Wilson's earlier speculation that she may have turned to fiction to ease the tensions of her mar-

riage. It is also reputed to have been the advice given her professionally by Dr. S. Weir Mitchell, a pioneer in female neuroses and himself a novelist. One is forced to conclude that American letters owe a great debt to Teddy.

Not only did Edith turn to writing; she also greatly increased and intensified her reading. She is certainly one of the most cultivated figures in our literature, although she never attended school or college. Before middle age she was able to write fiction in French, to translate (for publication) German into English, and to speak both these languages, as well as Italian, with complete facility. She made herself an expert in furniture, in decorating, in gardening. She was competently read in science, history, and philosophy. As an older woman she wore her learning with grace, but in these early years (and in view of the fact that she had developed it as an inner defense and without the example of other intellectuals) she must have sometimes allowed it to show a bit aggressively. In 1893 Paul Bourget, the French psychological novelist, came to Newport to gather material for a chapter on social life to be included in his book on the United States entitled *Outre-Mer*. In this chapter, which remains one of the few penetrating studies of that remarkable summer colony, he has a striking sketch of a type of woman that he labels the "intellectual tomboy." She:

> has read everything, understood everything, not superficially, but really, with an energy of culture that could put to shame the whole Parisian fraternity of letters. . . . Though like the others she gets her gowns from the best houses of the Rue de la Paix, there is not a book of Darwin, Huxley, Spencer, Renan, Taine, which she has not studied, not a painter or sculptor of whose works she could not compile a catalogue, not a school of poetry or romance of which she does not know the principles. . . . She subscribes impartially to the *Revue des Deux Mondes* and the gazettes of the latest coteries of the Latin Quarter or

Paul Bourget, Teddy, and Minnie Bourget in Edith's Panhard-Levassor, 1903 model, probably photographed by Edith. "The motor car has restored the romance of travel." *A Motor-Flight through France.*

Montmartre. Only she does not distinguish between them. She has not an idea that is not exact, yet she gives you a strange impression as if she had none. One would say that she has ordered her intellect somewhere, as we would order a piece of furniture, to measure, and with as many compartments as there are branches of human knowledge. She acquires them only that she may put them into these drawers. . . . Before the intellectual girl one longs to cry—"Oh, for one ignorance, one error, just a single one. May she make a blunder, may she prove not to know!" In vain. A mind may be mistaken, a mind may be ignorant, but never a thinking machine!

As Millicent Bell has pointed out, this description suggests much more an individual than a type. It is difficult to imagine that one would have run into many such "tomboys" in Newport. Besides, we know that Bourget did meet Edith on his visit there (they subsequently became great friends) and also that she was reading just these authors at the time. The woman whom Bourget describes is hardly charming, but I find it easy to imagine that Edith, frustrated by living entirely among the fashionable, should have let her erudition come hissing out like erupting lava at this welcome contact with a kindred soul. If it was rare to find a tomboy in Newport, it was even rarer to find a Bourget. In later years, when the presence of intellectuals in her drawing room was the rule rather than the exception, she would know better how to talk and to listen.

People, particularly women, always ask me if Edith had regrets about being childless. All I can say is that I have never come across any expression of it, written or quoted. Mrs. Chanler has said that she was afraid of children, and some who knew her when they were young have testified that she was stiff, or at the least reserved, with them. William R. Tyler, whose mother, Elesina Tyler, was Edith's last and closest friend, seems to have been the one person who, as a child, sensed the tremendous sympathy and buoyancy of her nature that was usually revealed only to adults. She made Tyler feel, as a school-boy in Harrow, that she was giving him in her letters the full measure of her mind, as though he were worthy of the most painstaking and time-consuming expression of her views. He loved her and called her "Edou."

But this was the wonderful Edith of later years. In the 1890s, I doubt that any child enjoyed such a companionship with her. Justine Cutting Ward has a girlhood memory of practicing the piano when her mother brought Mr. and Mrs. Wharton into the room to show them a tapestry. Naturally (in those days) she stopped playing and jumped to her feet, but no one addressed a word to her. As Mrs. Wharton left the room, however, she said to her husband in a clear voice: "Well, Teddy, it may be just as well that we never had children. Just think, one of them might have been musical!"

3

LITERARY BEGINNINGS

There were no such awkward moments as Justine Ward describes in the world that Edith was creating in her imagination. If, as a writer, she started late, she also started smoothly. Her first published story, "Mrs. Manstey's View," and "The Bunner Sisters" (not published until 1916 but apparently written at this time) are in the nature of literary exercises. Edith had set herself subjects as exercises: an old woman whose only remaining satisfaction in life is the contemplation of a backyard view, and a spinster proprietor of a notions shop who is reduced to ruin by her sister's disastrous marriage to an opium addict. She handles her themes competently, particularly in the second tale, but the reader is never more involved than the author. The details of the home lives of the miserable Bunners are graphically enough described, but we can never understand the attraction of both to the shabby, dope-taking clock repairman whom we see entirely through Edith's contemptuous vision. However, the narrative power which never failed her is already present.

Edith proceeded logically from publication in magazines to publication of books. Scribner's in 1899 and 1901 brought out two volumes of her short stories. The tales in *The Greater Inclination* and in *Crucial Instances* have some of the flavor of

Edith, publicity photograph.   57

James's stories of artists and writers of the same period. They are apt to be set against European backgrounds and to deal with such themes as the temptation to the serious artist of commercial success or the bewildering influence upon him of the art of an older, richer civilization. They are clever and readable, if a trifle thin, and in three of them, "The Pelican," "The Rembrandt," and "The Angel at the Grave," Edith shows herself already in full command of the style that was to make her prose as lucid and polished as any in American fiction. It is a firm, crisp, smooth, direct, easily flowing style, the perfect instrument of a clear, undazzled eye, an analytic mind, and a sense of humor alert to the least pretentiousness. We may later wonder if her style was adapted to all the uses to which she put it, but at this point it perfectly presents to us, in all their pathetic and confused dignity, the brave little lady who lectures with the boldness of ignorance to women's groups on arts and letters, first for the love of her baby but ultimately for the love of her own voice; the proud, splendid widow who is induced only by direst poverty to part with her false Rembrandt; and the dedicated spinster who devotes a lifetime to maintaining her grandfather's house as a shrine for a public that has forgotten him. The defect in Edith's poetry is that this same style, consciously ennobled and stripped of laughter, becomes dull and ornamental. Prose was always her natural instrument.

Her first novel, *The Valley of Decision*, appeared in 1902, when she was forty, and its scene is laid in Italy, that charnel house of English and American historical fiction. It is Edith's *Romola*, except that it is a better book than George Eliot's, for the fruits of her research are strewn attractively through the pages and not spooned into the reader like medicine. The discovery that she had made, in her travels with Teddy, of Italian eighteenth-century art, houses, furniture, was the prop on which the book rests. But although she captures remarkably the spirit and color of the century, nothing can save the novel from its pale and lifeless characters. It is like a play with perfect settings in which the actors stand stiffly in the middle of the stage, their eyes fixed on the prompter. Edith, as Edmund Wilson put it, was not only the pioneer but the poet of interior decoration.

She had done better when she had used this same scholarly knowledge more directly. The handbook, *The Decoration of Houses*, which she wrote in collaboration with the architect Ogden Codman, had a beneficent influence on the decorating and furnishing of the great private palaces of the 1890s. Its

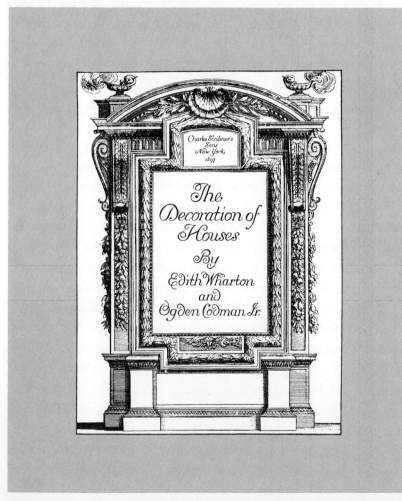

Title page of *The Decoration of Houses*, Edith's first book, 1897.

principal thesis was that the degeneration of interior decoration to gaudy fussiness had been caused by its divorce from the basic principles of architecture. Anyone today who takes the guided tours in Newport of those fantastic survivals of the gilded era—"The Breakers," "Marble House," "Belcourt"—will be glad to concede this. But Edith's book was for millionaires who wanted their Beaux Arts villas to be something more than merely ostentatious. It is of little use today except to a Greek shipper with an Aegean island to build on. The authors rather airily take for granted a classic taste and twenty servants. Hear them on dining rooms:

> Concerning the state dining room that forms a part of many modern houses little remains to be said beyond the descriptions already given of the various gala apartments. It is obvious that the banqueting-hall should be less brilliant than a ball-room and less fanciful in decoration than a music room: a severer and more restful treatment naturally suggests itself, but beyond this no special indications are required.

The eagerness with which Edith reached out to Paul Bourget in Newport is an indication of how greatly she thirsted for intellectual companionship. It was not easy to find. Even with her growing reputation as an author, she was too shy, too reticent, to break out of her group, and she always cared too much for sobriety and good manners to be at home in artistic circles. Besides, even if she had been able to conquer her reserve and to overlook Bohemian freedoms, she would still have had to reconcile Teddy to forays into fields which would have bored or disgusted him. The result, in the first dozen years of her marriage, while she was still living in the United States, was that she clung to the intellectual circle of a "few men of exceptional intelligence" who had at last "stirred the stagnant air of old New York" with the dust of new ideas: Egerton Winthrop,

Robert Minturn, Bayard Cutting, John Cadwalader, Walter Maynard, Stanford White, Ogden Codman, Walter Berry, Stephen Olin, George Rives.

Walter Van Rensselaer Berry.

Despite the presence of one or two big men on this list (Stanford White, for example), it has a distinct flavor of the aristocratic dilettante. Nobody was more aware of this than Edith herself. She noted that her friends were much given to social life, for which they all had marked gifts, and deplored the fact that so few of them made adequate use of their greater abilities. Of Egerton Winthrop she wrote that never had an intelligence so distinguished and a character so admirable been combined with interests so trivial. That she judged his type even more severely in her fiction than in her memoirs is attested by the long line of his prototypes in her stories: sterile, polished social parasites of perfect manners and little heart.

Walter Berry, a distant cousin and lifelong friend, was to become by far the most important of all these men in her life. There is even a legend that, as a debutante, she rejected his proposal of marriage. He was a lawyer, of wide and cultivated tastes, who ultimately settled in Paris where, as a charming, wise old bachelor, he came to know "everyone" in social, artistic, and diplomatic circles. He was a friend of Henry James and the dedicatee of Marcel Proust's *Pastiches et Mélanges*. At this time he was a frequent guest of the young Whartons in Newport, and it was during one of these visits that Edith showed him the "lumpy pages" of an early manuscript and had the mortification of hearing his shout of laughter, a peal that was never quite to cease ringing in her ears. But a minute later he said good-naturedly: "Come, let's see what can be done," and settled down beside her to model the lump into a book. In that modeling process she claimed that she had been taught whatever she knew about the writing of "clear, concise English."

I hardly believe this, although I am sure that she did. There seemed no limits to her admiration of Berry. "He found me when my mind and soul were hungry and thirsty, and he fed me till our last hour together." Few of her friends agreed with this high estimate. To Percy Lubbock, Berry was a dogmatic

62

Howard Sturgis with a younger friend on the steps of Qu'Acre, Windsor, England.

and snobbish egotist, the evil genius, indeed, of her life. "None of her friends," he put it bluntly, "thought that she was the better for the surrender of her fine free spirit to the control of a man, I am ready to believe, of strong intelligence and ability—but also, I certainly know, of a dry and narrow and supercilious temper."

In later years, after Edith's divorce, some of her friends were to judge Berry malicious and spiteful for not marrying her. It was even said that it was his revenge for her earlier, legendary rejection of his suit. But I incline to the position that Edith was satisfied with the friendship that he offered. Their relationship does not suggest a love affair to me. If they had had a happy one, why would they not have married when she obtained her freedom in 1913? And if they had had an unhappy one, would their intense friendship have continued, unabated, until Berry's death in 1928? Edith's greatest friendships were always with men: Henry James, Howard Sturgis, Percy Lubbock, John Hugh-Smith, Robert Norton. This does not mean that she did not have women friends, too, for, of course, she did: Mrs. Chanler, Mrs. Tyler, Mrs. R. W. Bliss, to name but three, but I believe that she had an intenser intellectual communion with the opposite sex, and one that had no necessary sexual relation. Edith never put her spirit in Berry's "control," or, for that matter, in anyone else's. She was far too independent. It is a common error to assume that most human relationships consist of a dominator and a dominated. Edith was entirely capable of selecting what she wanted from Berry's copious imagination without binding herself to take it all. Even granting that he was a snob, a gossip, and a materialist, does that have to mean that he could not be the subtlest of critics, the most sympathetic of human companions? I think not.

An early story (1893), "The Fullness of Life," which Edith never included in any volume of tales, may be a sketch of what she hoped, ideally, to be offered by Berry and of what she hoped, vainly, to be offered by Teddy. I dare to speculate that this story may have come right out of a session with a psychiatrist. It is faintly embarrassing to read, as is all early fiction where the author's daydreaming is exposed. A frustrated intellectual woman, whose husband's creaking boots symbolize his total rejection of the world of art and beauty, dies and discovers that she may select a new soul mate for eternity. She is about to choose an aesthete as exquisite as herself when she learns that her husband, on dying, will now also have to choose a new mate, and she decides, after all, to wait for him. Those creaking boots have become the symbol of a human love which transcends aesthetic enjoyment.

The story is grossly sentimental and quite unlike any other that she published. She must have been trying to persuade herself that Teddy's love, the love of an honest and devoted, if uninteresting man, was worth all the arty chatter of a hundred Winthrops and Berrys. But it wasn't, and she knew it wasn't, because Teddy was not that much of a man. If she was to get love from neither, she might at least have picked the man who could talk.

Edith never lost this romantic sense of what a "real man" might be, but she did not fully realize him in her fiction until *Hudson River Bracketed*, when she was old. We see a sketch of him in John Amherst, the vigorous, uncompromising social reformer in *The Fruit of the Tree*, of blunted sensitivity but of passionate heart and loyalty, with a head like Schiller's. Ah, yes, what woman would not forgive the absence of subtlety in such a lover! But even Amherst lacks the basic guts to stand behind his second wife, a nurse, when she is in trouble over a thoroughly justified mercy killing. Even he takes his ultimate stand in the chilly line of Edith's heroes: men of good taste, good manners, and attenuated will power.

There is, however, a distinction that should be made between these heroes: Lawrence Selden in *The House of Mirth*,

George Darrow in *The Reef*, who are men to some degree capable of loving and being loved, and the dry, older, nonhero, gentleman dilettantes who appear in so many of the novels and stories: Mr. Langhope in *The Fruit of the Tree*, Fraser Leath of *The Reef*, Culwin in "The Eyes." These latter, with whom I identify Winthrop and even Berry, are loveless, usually unlovable, and capable at times of being actually cruel and malicious. This is most dramatically brought out in "The Eyes." Culwin tells a listening group about a fire, which includes his young protégé, of the eyes, the old eyes with sunk orbits and thick, red-lined lids and look of vicious security that haunt him at night whenever he has performed an unselfish act, which the reader, of course, knows to be just the opposite. As he finishes his tale, he marks the horror on the features of the protégé, with whose youth and bloom he has tried to water his own dry nature, and turning to look in the mirror behind him, he sees at last whose eyes they are.

How, the reader of this study may ask, in view of the solemn eulogiums that Edith wrote of Berry do I dare imagine that his image was even dimly in her mind when she created · Culwin? Because I know that such a characterization is perfectly consistent with the deepest friendship that a novelist can feel. Edith herself, in *Hudson River Bracketed*, would create a wholly sympathetic novelist character who deliberately uses every emotional experience, however personal, however intimate, as grist for his fictional mill. She knew that thus novels are made.

Stairway in the Ogden Mills house at Staatsburg, New York, reputed to have suggested the one at Bellomont in *The House of Mirth*, where Lily Bart pauses to look down at the house party and to sense the futility of her life.

4

THE HOUSE OF MIRTH

The House of Mirth, published in 1905 and an immediate best seller, marks Edith's coming of age as a writer. She had at last the perfect subject: fashionable New York. "There it was before me," she wrote, "in all its flatness and futility, asking to be dealt with as the theme most available to my hand, since I had been steeped in it from infancy." Her only doubt was whether she could extract from a study of irresponsible pleasure seekers any significance deeper than the pleasure which they sought, but her doubt was resolved with the realization that she could find dramatic significance in society's power of debasing people and ideals.

She saw the new rich, the post-Civil War millionaires, the "lords of Pittsburgh," whom she dubbed the "invaders," as the peculiarly corrupting force. Their limitless fortunes and equally limitless vulgarity seemed to sweep away not only old standards of taste and decorum but old standards of morality. But the "invaded," the forces of her old brownstone, genteel New York, made love to the invaders. That was Edith's particular insight: that the old and new, having at heart the same materialist philosophy, were bound to be reconciled. It was all very well for Henry James, in *The American Scene*, to describe the Newport of his childhood, surviving into this gilded age, as a little bare white open hand suddenly crammed with gold, but the fingers of that little hand closed firmly enough over the proffered bullion. Edith saw that invaders and invaded would bury the hatchet in a noisy, stamping dance, and she saw also the pathos of the individual who was fated to be trampled under the feet of those boisterous truce makers—the pathos of her heroine, Lily Bart.

Lily stems from both worlds. Her father is related to the old New York Penistons and the Stepneys, but is driven by her mother, of more ordinary origins, to make a fortune which, not being of invader blood, he is bound to lose. Lily, orphaned, is loosed on the social seas with only her beauty and charm for sails and no rudder but a ladylike disdain for shabby compromises and a vague sense that there must be somewhere a better life than the one into which she has drifted. Her rich friends, who use her as a social secretary to write notes and as a blind to shield them from importunate and suspicious husbands, cannot understand the squeamishness which keeps her, at the critical moment, from extracting a proposal from the rich bachelor whom she has not been too squeamish to pursue. Her respectable relatives, on the other hand, of an older society, cannot understand her smoking or gambling or being seen, however briefly, in the company of married men. Lily falls between two stools. She cannot bring herself to marry the coarse Mr. Rosedale for all his millions, or the obscure Lawrence Selden, for all their affinity. She postpones decisions and hopes for the best and in the meanwhile seeks to distract herself. But we know from the start that she is doomed. The other characters, of both new and old New York, seem strangely and vindictively united in a constant readiness to humiliate her: Grace Stepney to tell tales on her, Mrs. Peniston to disinherit her, Bertha Dorset to abandon her in a foreign port, Gus Trenor to try to seduce her, his wife to say he has. And in the end when she finally compromises and is willing to marry Rosedale, it is too late. He will not have her, and she falls to the

70

Edith smoking in Lenox, Massachusetts, 1905. In *The House of Mirth*, published that same year, Lily Bart is careful to conceal her smoking from eligible suitors.

job at the milliner's and the ultimate overdose of sleeping tablets. But we finish the book with the conviction that in the whole brawling, terrible city Lily is the one and only lady.

The different levels of society in *The House of Mirth* are explored with a precision comparable to that of Proust, whom Edith was later so greatly to admire. We follow Lily's gradual descent from Bellomont on the Hudson and the other great country houses of a world where the old and new societies had begun to merge, to the little court of the Gormers, who, although rich enough to be ultimately accepted, are still at the stage of having to fill their house with hangers-on, to the bogus intellectual world of Carry Fisher, who pretends to like interesting people while she earns her living helping climbers up the social ladder, to the final drop into the gilded hotel of the demimondaine Norma Hatch. Lily learns that money is the greatest common denominator of all these worlds and that the differences between them consist only in the degrees of scent with which its odor is from time to time concealed. Van Wyck Brooks accused Edith of knowing nothing of the American West, and perhaps she did not, but she had a firsthand knowledge of where the profits of the frontier had gone. Lily Bart, weary on foot, watching the carriages and motors of her former friends ply up and down Fifth Avenue, Mrs. Van Osburgh's C-spring barouche, Mrs. Hatch's electric victoria, is seeing the natural successors of the covered wagon.

Blake Nevius has suggested that *The House of Mirth* belongs with the novels of the period that explored the waste of human and spiritual resources that in America went hand in hand with the exploitation of the land and forests. I would use a stronger word than waste. It is deliberate destruction. What explains the continuing fascination of this novel is not the moral struggle but the drama of the hunt of a desperate creature by a pack of remorseless hounds. The creature may double back in her tracks, she may bound over streams, and occasionally her pursuers may lose the scent, but so does she lose strength and speed, and the end is inevitable. She never has a chance. She is too beautiful. Lily's beauty is the light in which each of her different groups would like to shine, but when they find that it illuminates their ugliness they want to put it out. It is a beauty, however, that is indestructible, even in poverty, even in death, a beauty that the Trenors and Dorsets, with all their taste and money and ingenuity, can never hope to duplicate, a beauty that is the haunting symbol of what society might be—and isn't.

It is possible to read Lily's whole story in the changes of her appearance. When we first see her, through Selden's eyes, in

Illustration from *The House of Mirth*. Lily Bart sweeps by, unconscious of the scornful stare of the cleaning woman who has misconstrued her visit to a bachelor's apartment.

Grand Central Station, she is beginning to lose her purity of tint after eleven years of late hours and dancing, yet everything about her is still "rigorous and exquisite, at once strong and fine." It strikes Selden that she must have cost a great deal to make, as if numbers of dull and ugly people had been sacrificed to produce her. Not until he sees her in her last great social triumph, as Sir Joshua Reynolds' Mrs. Lloyd in a *tableau vivant* at the Brys', with poised foot and lifted arm, all "soaring grace," is the full poetry of her loveliness revealed to him. Then he sees her as divested of the trivialities of her world and catching "a note of that eternal harmony of which her beauty was part."

As adversity deepens, Selden notices a subtle alteration in her looks. They have lost the transparency through which fluctuations of the spirit are sometimes tragically visible and have fused into a hard, brilliant substance. Later, at the reading of Mrs. Peniston's disinheriting will, we see her "tall and noble in her black dress." Rosedale meets her in the street, drooping with lassitude, and is struck by the way the dark penciling of fatigue under her eyes and the morbid, blue-veined pallor of her temples bring out the brightness of her hair and lips. He sees her beauty as a "forgotten enemy" that has lain in ambush to spring out on him unawares. And Selden, watching her for the last time kneeling on the hearthrug, will remember long afterward "how the red play of the flame sharpened the depression of her nostrils, and intensified the blackness of the shadows which struck up from her cheekbones to her eyes." A few hours later he is to see her on her narrow bed, "with motionless hands and calm, unrecognizing face, the semblance of Lily Bart."

Edith. Publicity photograph.

5

FRIENDSHIPS

Edith, particularly on her long sojourns in Europe, was now beginning to meet the literary people she wanted. It is interesting to note that as she replaced the old New York circle with a European one, she retained some of the dilettante quality of the first. The new members were more professionally involved in the world of letters, and they no longer had business or legal affiliations, but they were all still gentlemen, and inclined more to criticism than creation. Howard Sturgis, son of the American banker in London, Russell Sturgis, was the center of Edith's British circle. He was a witty and caustic bachelor who did embroidery work and wrote one very fine novel, *Belchamber*. He entertained delightfully in his roomy, comfortable house in Windsor, "Queen's Acre," abbreviated to "Qu'Acre." Through him Edith came to know Percy Lubbock, novelist and critic, Gaillard Lapsley, American-born Cambridge don, Robert Norton, diplomat and water-colorist, John Hugh-Smith, book collector. It was a somewhat epicene group of bachelors (Lubbock alone among them ever married, and he not until middle age), but it supplied Edith at last with the true sympathy and understanding that she so strongly needed.

There was a mighty exception to the dilettante aspect of Sturgis's group. Henry James was the one great artist whom

Howard Sturgis's house, Qu'Acre, Windsor, England.

Edith could call an intimate friend. She adored him, cultivated him, pursued him. She would descend upon him in Lamb House in her motor and whisk him away on sight-seeing jaunts or lure him to her apartment in Paris for what he described as her "succulent and corrupting meals." He returned her devotion—

ABOVE: Land's End, Edith and Teddy's second home in Newport. OPPOSITE: Henry James. Caricature by Sir Max Beerbohm. "The Old Diner-Out."

or most of it—but he was inclined to fret at her interruptions of his sacred routine. Half-playfully, half-ruefully, he likened her to a golden eagle with a beautiful genius for great globe adventures, by whose side he was nothing but "a poor old croaking barnyard fowl." "I have simply lain stretched," he wrote her, on hearing of a motor trip in Tunisia, "a faithful old veteran slave, upon the doormat of your palace of adventure." It is amusing to note that behind all the hyperbole of their exchanged

The Old Diner-Out.

a Memory.

æt
1926

compliments, Edith and Henry cared more for each other as persons than as writers. She found his later novels more and more severed from the nourishing air in which men must live and breathe, and he thought her books best when (like *The Reef*) they were most like his own.

In all the bulky literature about James I know of no memoir that makes him come more alive than his two allotted chapters in *A Backward Glance*. Edith's description of him has been called "catty," but I think it would seem so only to an unhumorous and too solemnly worshiping Jacobite. The "master" could indeed be fussy, labored, falsely modest, self-cherishing, and obsessed with the rules of his own very special art which he applied too widely to that of others. Why should he not be shown that way, so long as the greatness of his soul and talent are also demonstrated? I cherish the picture of James on Edith's terrace in Lenox reaching back in his memory to evoke, from a fog of ejaculations, epithets, and parenthetical rectifications, a train of ghosts of long-dead Emmet cousins, who suddenly flashed as vividly as Ingres drawings before the listener, and another equally memorable but frankly comic picture of him sweating in the New England summer heat, an electric fan clutched in one

OPPOSITE: Drawing room at Land's End looking out to sea. ABOVE: Library at Land's End.

hand, a pile of sucked oranges at his elbow, a mountain of misery, a woebegone bear.

The sketch, however, that the reader of Edith's memoirs keeps filling in for himself is that of Edith looking at James; it is the contrast between the sketcher and her subject that gives half the fun to these chapters. We see the all-efficient Edith with the always procrastinating Henry, she ready to go, he constantly lingering, she summing up every problem in a word, he gasping in further involutions, she extravagant, he frugal, she masculine when he was feminine, and very feminine when he was most masculine. It is an enchanting contrast, and it enchanted them.

BELOW: Edith, Henry James, and Teddy starting on "a motor-flight through France" in Edith's Panhard in 1907. Teddy, characteristically, sits up forward with the chauffeur. The baggage was sent on by van to hotels.
OPPOSITE: The garden room at Lamb House, Rye, England, where Henry James dictated the great novels of his final period. This room was destroyed by a bomb in World War II, but has been reconstructed.

Teddy.

How often we hear the phrase "like something out of Henry James or Edith Wharton"! There is a tendency to regard her as a disciple, and, in her detractors, as a rather pale imitation of the great man. But we see in her memoirs that they had little fundamentally in common but the fact, admittedly an important one, that both were expatriated Americans. Even their mutual personal admiration was not always a sure thing. She speculated that he might have found her visits to Lamb House more of a burden than a pleasure, and, indeed, he regarded her as the "angel of devastation," and the speed with which he took advantage of her motor to tour the countryside seems to imply an eagerness to get at least *that* advantage from her visits. But what never failed was their fascination for, and, I suspect, their occasional envy of, each other. There is a charming picture in Percy Lubbock's *Portrait of Edith Wharton* of James making gentle fun of her at Queen's Acre when Howard Sturgis reads aloud from *Ethan Frome* a remark of the fictitious narrator: "I had been sent by my employers . . .":

How Henry James caught at the words, with his great round stare of drollery and malice at the suggested image—of Edith *sent*, and sent by *employers*! What a power of invention it implied in her to think of that!

Another of Edith's cherished Panhards.

6

DIVORCE

Edith's mother died in 1901, and she came into her last family inheritance. She and Teddy were now rich enough to afford a more splendid residence than they had heretofore had, and they commissioned Francis L. V. Hoppin to design a country house in Lenox, Massachusetts. The author of *The Decoration of Houses*, needless to say, knew precisely what she wanted. Edith had selected Belton House in England, a Christopher Wren creation, as her model, and she restored the cupola and balustrade that had been removed in a later renovation. The Mount (named for Edith's patriotic military ancestor's home), a large, white symmetrical three-story structure with two wings, was placed on an elevation where it could regally command her formal gardens. Both she and Teddy loved it, but she never loved it enough not to quit it for Europe.

Every year now produced another and different kind of dazzling success for Edith. *The Fruit of the Tree* (1907) showed that she was not confined to society, that she could write a vigorous tale about a factory manager who sought to improve the lives of his exploited operators. *Ethan Frome* (1911) demonstrated that she could deal expertly with knotty New England characters who were as far removed socially from The Mount as they must have been geographically close. In 1912 she pro-

Belton House, Lincolnshire, England, designed by Sir Christopher Wren and used by the architect, Francis L. V. Hoppin, as the model for The Mount.

duced an exquisite Jamesian novel, *The Reef*, centered about a French château, shimmering in color yet clean of line, like a painting by Walter Gay, and the following year she offered *The Custom of the Country*, a determinist novel in the manner of Zola. In 1908 and 1910 came collections of short stories. It was small wonder that Teddy appeared to Consuelo Vanderbilt Balsan as a kind of cipher in Edith's life, "as more of an equerry than an equal, walking behind her and carrying whatever paraphernalia she happened to discard." He was not surviving happily into the years of her fame.

Edith's letters to Walter and Eunice Maynard, New York (and originally Lenox) friends, reflect her growing concern over

The Mount, Lenox, Massachusetts.

Library at The Mount.

Garden stairway at The Mount.

Teddy's increased detachment from her life. At first he is part
of the general frenzy of speed and sight-seeing. She writes
Eunice in 1906:

> Speaking of "zipping," please tell Mr. Maynard
> that about a month ago (in London) Teddy bought
> a second-hand 15 h.p. Panhard, and that since then
> we have not only "scoured the plain" like "swift
> Camilla," but climbed mountains and descended preci-
> pices, without being sick or sorry for a moment. We
> raced around England for a fortnight, and then, dis-
> couraged by the bitter cold, came back to the conti-
> nent, and starting at Boulogne, rushed through
> Normandy and Touraine down to this beautiful, won-
> derful Auvergne, one of the most enchanting motor-
> grounds one can imagine—if only the rain did not
> pursue us! It has been a cold, dark dreary spring in
> Europe, owing to Vesuvius, they say.

The letter reads like a paean to the automobile. It is almost as if the Whartons were trying to submerge their marital troubles in speed. Edith contrasts the celerity of growth of the Maynards' baby, Walter, Jr., with that of a Panhard and speaks of her congratulatory letter on the latter's birth as "coming halting after, like a well-meaning but tardy Cadillac." But in the next few years the pace of their traveling was slowed down by Teddy's deteriorating mental and physical health, though his recuperations were promptly marked by a resumption of motoring. When Edith returned from one of her solo trips to Europe, she found that Teddy was not at The Mount. He was better enough physically to have bought himself a motor and driven the hundred miles from Lenox to Groton. "A few months ago

OPPOSITE: Albi Cathedral, "a hairless pink monster that has just crawled up from the river to bask on the cliff." *A Motor-Flight through France.*
BELOW: Carcassonne, famous medieval castle reconstructed by the controversial Viollet-le-Duc. "The universal restorer has for once been justified by his results." *A Motor-Flight through France.*

he would have said this was impossible," she observed. The winter of 1910 found them still traveling:

> Poor Teddy, who left New York in blooming condition, developed gout on the voyage and had a bad attack on arriving. He rounded it off with a nasty grippe, and this "settled" into facial neuralgia, which has driven him almost wild. He isn't the best and most angelic of invalids, and I've been actively engaged in trying to make him forget his woes by the charms of my conversation and companionship. In point of health, this year, we've really been like the lady and gentleman in the barometer; and I think he thinks it's *my* turn now to turn green, or whatever happens, when the weather goes wrong! Mr. D. packed him off to the south as soon as he could, and we've been flying over Provence in that amazing old car, which really has a "temperament" compared to which Ninon de l'Enclos's wasn't worth mentioning! Please tell Mr. Maynard that we made the run from Avignon to Hyères in 4 hours and 50 minutes!

Teddy was not well enough to return to The Mount that summer; he was now showing more distinctly the symptoms of the nervous crack-up that was to cloud the rest of his life. Edith writes to Walter Maynard:

> I'm so glad things are going well with you, and that there's a chance of seeing you here. The doctors won't let us return for the summer, as Teddy's sister is not going back to Lenox, and they think it would be too isolated for me, and the place too much of a care, as I have to be so constantly with Teddy. We are over here for a few days' rest and change for me, and to see Mr. James, who is close by at Rye; but we return next week, and you will find us at 53 rue de Varenne in June, probably, if you come out, as I hope you will. Teddy is on the whole rather better, and so

Chateau de Grignan, Provence, where Madame de Sévigné's son-in-law "dispensed an almost royal hospitality and ruled with more than royal arrogance." *A Motor-Flight through France.*

pleased with the apartment, and our quiet pottering life there, that the doctors think we had better stay there for the present. I showed him your letter, and he was so pleased with it. It would be a great pleasure to him to see you and Eunice. He *seemed* well when you saw him last summer but, alas, was *not.* But his family would not recognize it, in spite of my letters and warnings.

The marriage might have held together had Teddy been the strong man that Edith must have initially visualized. But he wasn't. He was not only weak; he was neurasthenic. He was like a child in his retaliations against the precious literary circle whose elaborate and factitious friendliness he must have immediately seen through. He had girl friends now and boasted about it. Perhaps even, horror of horrors, to Henry James!

93

Amiens Cathedral, "like some mysteriously preserved ancestor of the human race, some Wandering Jew grown sedentary and throned in stony contemplation." *A Motor-Flight through France.*

Mrs. Chanler related to me that on one of her motor trips with Edith they stopped at a hotel in a town that neither of them had previously visited. As they were signing the register, Edith noted the prior entry of a "Mr. and Mrs." Edward R. Wharton, and observed with a slight smile and shrug: "Evidently I *have* been here before."

The great Henry and the bachelor friends, Howard Sturgis and Gaillard Lapsley, threw up their hands in horror at this new Teddy. "Dear Edith's" life had turned to hell! But what could they do but silently sympathize? As James put it, he could neither hold Edith's hand nor kick Teddy's tail. We may be permitted, however, to speculate that James's idea of hell was a more temperate zone than ours. Teddy in his decline must have been a cruel trial for a woman of Edith's sensitivity and pride, but I imagine that he was less of a trial for her than he would have been for James. Women are apt to be tougher than fastidious old bachelors, and, besides, Edith had the mighty compensations of her own great talent, now in its finest bloom.

I suggest that Edith's "hell" of this period was less in the humiliation which Teddy's conduct caused her than in the agony of her own decision to divorce him. Divorce was not admitted in the New York of her childhood, and this New York had molded her conscience. Edith was nothing if not dutiful. Her letters are filled with references to her obligations, financial and otherwise, to her servants, to old retainers of her family, to friends in trouble, to relatives. She may have been possessive, but hers was a benevolent, protective possessiveness. We see her pounding the chancelleries for information about missing persons, engaging cars for indigent relatives, pulling wires for prizes and honors for those she felt were deserving. Now what would be such a woman's idea of her own duty to an ailing husband but to take him back to the home that he loved and cherish him there? Would this have meant the sacrifice of her writing? Certainly not. It would have entailed only the sacrifice of the trappings of a literary life.

But these she could not bring herself to give up. She had found Europe; she had found, belatedly, congenial friends. Teddy was unfaithful, abusive, violent, impossible. No modern woman would have hesitated to shed him. But Edith was not a modern woman. She must have been tortured by the idea that she *ought* to be stifling in Lenox with her ridiculous mate. If he was ridiculous, might she not have made him so? Still, she had to choose. In 1910 she had moved permanently to France. In 1913 she got her divorce. Teddy's family were to hate her for it, ever after, but, much more importantly, I wonder if she did not a bit hate herself. To a woman of her intense conscience the price of freedom must have been terrible. Nor was there any real help for her, in her decision, from anyone else. She looked from the weak Teddy to the dry Walter. Small wonder that one of her perennial problems as a novelist was that she was never able to create a real man as a hero. Had she known any?

In this troubled period of Edith's life, there should have been something to console her in the aspirations of other women. Her sex everywhere were refusing to be confined to the home;

Edith, equestrienne.

96

they were demanding the vote and the right to have a say in the management of their own lives. Divorce had ceased to be a social disgrace even in Newport where Mrs. William K. Vanderbilt was able to shed her husband and marry Oliver H. P. Belmont without impairing her position. But Edith's attitude in these matters was always ambivalent. For all her force of character, she never shook off the firm sense of propriety of old brownstone New York imbued in her by her mother and grandmother. A lady was never free to kick over forms. Even if Edith had to procure a divorce, she could never really regard herself as a "divorced woman."

The same ambivalence can be seen in her fiction. Although her sympathy goes out to many of her women characters who seek release from intolerable marriages, she always makes them pay a heavy price for their freedom, and she distinctly implies that it is better for them that there should be such payment. For example, Mrs. Lidcote in "Autre Temps" discovers that New York society, which has tolerated in her daughter conduct for which she herself was ostracized a generation earlier, will still not reinstate her. It is too busy to revise old judgments. What is fascinating about this story is that the author obviously feels that the rejected mother has a deeper and better life than the easily accepted daughter. The price of divorce *must* be suffering. Edith was a gilded puritan.

Here is how I should sum up the story of her marriage: she and Teddy were married at a time when she had no reason to believe that she would not always be satisfied with the social life of the New York society matron whose spouse Teddy seemed perfectly qualified to be. This life rapidly bored her, and Teddy, a neurasthenic, lacked the ability either to dominate her or to interest her. She took up traveling, decorating, and finally writing to compensate for the frustrations of her married life, and in so doing she discovered that she was made for a totally different existence. Teddy's near-lunatic temper and their childless-

ness made a bad situation impossible. In the end the only thing she could do was to cut loose and start afresh, in a new country, without a spouse. Who in 1971 can cast the first stone at her?

When it was all over at last, she wrote to the Maynards:

> Your letter touched me very much. I tried to write to a few of my friends about the situation, but somehow the ghastly reiteration was more than I could stand, and I didn't get very far! I appreciate all you say, and I think the people who have seen and known the situation most continuously for the last year or two will understand that I did what I could. My chief sensation now is one of utter weariness. I suppose I shall come to life again before long, but at present I'm rather numb. I have been trying to take a semi-rest-cure here, not having the energy to go away; but Paris during the New York season is rather over-whelming if one doesn't feel well, and I am tantalized at being surrounded by friends, and not feeling up to seeing them except in short glimpses.

It seems appropriate to close this discussion of Edith's divorce with a picture of how the constantly present inward satisfaction of having achieved some part of her literary goal operated to relieve the strains of life with Teddy. In a letter from Queen's Acre, Windsor, to Walter Berry in 1908 she exclaimed: "Ye Gods! When I went to bed last night I said to myself, 'It is no use, nothing helps'." Any desperate hope, she wrote, that the machine of her life was running again always turned out to be an illusion: it was only the crank whirring round and round. But the very next day a wonderful thing happened. She and Henry James drove over to call on George Meredith and found on his table a copy of her latest book: *A Motor-Flight through France*. At first Meredith did not know who she was, but when James shouted in his deaf ears that his visitor was Edith Wharton, the *writer*, the great man dragged himself upright in his chair,

Teddy and canine friends.   99 stretched out both hands, and held Edith's in a long pressure while he murmured: "Wharton? Wharton? Is this *Mrs.* Wharton? Why, my dear child, I've read every word you've written, and I always wanted to know you! Come close so that I can look at you and see what you are like. But is it really you? Why, I was flying through France in your motor only a moment ago!" Edith ends her letter by saying that when she got back to Queen's Acre, she repeated the words over and over to herself so that she might remember them forever.

7

THE CUSTOM OF THE COUNTRY

The year that brought Edith her freedom, 1913, also saw the publication of *The Custom of the Country*, whose protagonist, Undine Spragg, twice ruthlessly divorces blameless husbands for personal advantage. But if Edith identified herself in this respect with Undine—as a kind of psychological punishment—it was the only way she did. Her novel is a fierce indictment of the mindless materialism that she felt was infecting American life, and Undine Spragg is this evil force incarnate. She is a beautiful, vivid creature, but made of alloy, and as sentimental in judging herself as she is ruthless in judging others. A father is nothing to her but a checkbook, a husband a means of social advancement, a baby a threat to the figure. No amount of exposure to cultivated persons can ripple the surface of her infinite vulgarity. She never knows the toll in human misery of her advance to the social heights, for she never looks back. The past ceases to exist for her. The story of how she hews her way through the old New York ranks of the Marvells and Dagonets, already weakened by prior compromises with the "invaders" (*The House of Mirth*) and even into the closed society of the Faubourg Saint-Germain in Paris, is fascinating. Undine gets into more dangerous corners than Lily Bart, but by miscalculation rather than inertia, and the same shrewd, restless cerebration that gets her in can be counted on to get her out. In *The*

House of Mirth our compassion goes out to Lily; in *The Custom of the Country* it goes out to the society which Undine is trying to crash.

Edith is really embattled now against the invaders. They have come much further than they were in *The House of Mirth*. They are a disease that has contaminated all of New York society, as witnessed by the startling fact that they no longer need charm or cultivation or even much money to encompass their ends. Undine's success is a uniquely American phenomenon. She has nothing but her looks and her greed. She is ignorant and insensitive, devoid of passion or maternal instinct, but with a lot of brass and a bit of luck she can make it. Her success speaks more for the weakness of the patient than for the virulence of the microbe.

The Marvells, family of her first victim Ralph, are actually richer than the Spraggs. They are established and respected, whereas the Spraggs are encamped precariously in an unfashionable West Side hotel. But Ralph has no energy. He is self-consciously and complacently of "aboriginal New York." His forebears, whose traditions he can never forget, have enjoyed "a tranquil disdain for money getting" and a "passive openness to the finer sensations." The fatal mistake, which will ultimately lead him to suicide, is that he takes Undine's ignorance for innocence and her selfishness for vigor. There is something almost decadent in so willful a misconstruction. Nor is it the first such mistake in his family. His cousin, Clare, has married invader Peter Van Degen and has learned to repent, but she, at least, has repented in the Van Degen diamonds, while the Van Degen motor bears "her broken heart from opera to ball." For Ralph there will be no such compensations.

He will not even have a happy honeymoon. With a terrible insight Edith understood that women like Undine regarded intimacy as a pretext for escaping from the forms of worldly intercourse into a total absence of expression. Undine's parents,

Edith, publicity photograph.

for example, "seldom spoke to each other when they met, and words of greeting seemed almost unknown to their domestic vocabulary." Under the simplified social code of the Spraggs and of other denizens of gaudy West Side emporiums called The Malibran or The Stentorian, the amenities are reduced to a handful of platitudes, crude jokes, and expressions of complaint or self-assertion. Yet these people threaten to turn the world into a replica of their own hideous habitations.

In a determinist novel the ending should flow inevitably from the given facts of the opening situation. The author should simply have to place the Spraggs in juxtaposition with the Marvells, and the latter should be devoured. Edith never, to my knowledge, described *The Custom of the Country* as a determinist novel, so there is no reason to judge it by Zola's standards, but as it appears to be one and as it gives an awesome effect of ineluctable circumstance, it may be permissible to point out the role that coincidence actually plays in the plot. Would Ralph Marvell have been too disdainful of the chicanery of shyster lawyers in a "quickie divorce" state to have lost custody of his son by mere default? Would he have committed suicide on learning that his *ex*-wife had been secretly married and divorced before she had married him? Is that not carrying his sensitivity too far? And would the Marquis de Chelles have married a penniless American woman of clouded reputation such as Undine? Surely French aristocrats of that era, like Ralph's cousin Clare, at least received coin for their compromise.

I point these things out to show that Edith had to stack her cards in favor of her protagonist. She had actually gone too far in her assumption that it was a Spragg world. The society that destroyed Lily Bart might still have had claws to take care of Undine. But it hardly matters, for Undine was the future. By the 1920s she would have it all her way. A more important fault in the book is Edith's failure to be more explicit about Undine's sexuality. A determinist novel is aided by the franker methods

104

of Zola. I should like some bedroom scenes in *The Custom of the Country*. After all, Edith has made it clear that sex is Undine's only weapon in the battle for social supremacy. She lacks education, charm, good temper, social background, and wealth. Surely it is vital to the story of her rise to know how she uses her body —particularly as it is strongly suggested that even in this respect she is a cheat. Peter Van Degen deserts her; the Marquis de Chelles takes to other women. The supreme irony of Undine's story is that her only asset is the appearance of one. She is no good in bed. Lily Bart might have been.

It is this that makes the ending of the novel so magnificent. Undine, like Macbeth, has it all: abounding wealth, fabulous jewels, palaces everywhere, and a social circle that includes anyone she wants. The language of the last chapter reads like that of a ladies' magazine—or like the mind of Undine. But the famous exception to Undine's bliss that sours the taste of her victory— her disqualification, as a divorcée, ever to become an ambassadress, which is now, of course, the only thing she wants—is not the real twist of the finale. That lies in the reduction of Elmer Moffatt, Undine's first and fourth husband, the tycoon of tycoons, the invader *par excellence*, to the rank of the other two, Marvell and Chelles. For Elmer is already dissatisfied with his selfish bride who has no time to give to her only child and who is already finding Elmer vulgar. He has stolen the world to throw it in Undine's lap, and she is no more grateful for it than she was for Ralph Marvell's entrée into New York society or Chelles's into the old Faubourg. So in the end the invaders themselves fall victim to the triumphant Genghis Khan of American commercial society: the sexless female who knows nothing and believes in nothing, but who holds the world strictly accountable for her eternal disappointments.

8

PARIS AND WAR

In *Madame de Treymes,* an earlier novelette of Jamesian inspiration, Edith had shown an idealistic young American, a spiritual heir of the master's Christopher Newman, victimized by the sophisticated world of the Faubourg Saint-Germain. Undine Spragg turned the tables on this world. From this point on in Edith's fiction the wind from the west brought no aromas of innocence to a wicked, older civilization. The forest primeval of Longfellow had been cut down by adventurers from whose aggression Europeans would need all their wit to protect themselves. Edith had switched her own sympathies in moving across the Atlantic.

When she wrote a series of articles during the First World War, designed to acquaint American soldiers coming to France with the character of their Gallic allies and hosts, she emphasized the French qualities of taste, reverence, continuity, and intellectual honesty. This picture of the *grande nation,* chained to ancient forms and observances, is hardly that of a country which survived four years of savage trench warfare with the first military power of Europe. But Edith was paying France the greatest compliment that she knew in describing as national virtues those of its qualities that most attracted her. We can read some of the self-justification of the expatriate in her attitude

World War I poster. Imperial Germany as it appeared to Edith and Henry James.

107

that her adopted country had to possess to the fullest and her native land to the least, the civilized, cultivated atmosphere that she craved. As a result, there was always a presumption in favor of France in her thinking, just as there was one against America, an injustice that is everywhere reflected in these articles. When she speaks of French culture, she invokes Richelieu and the Academy; when it is a question of American, she cites only the Middle Western college girl who "learnt art" in a year.

She now lived in an apartment on the Rue de Varenne in the Faubourg Saint-Germain, near the Invalides. Just down the street was the magnificent Hôtel Biron, occupied by the sculptor Rodin, whose garden was James's model for the site where Strether in *The Ambassadors* has his vision of his wasted American life and his spiritual rebirth. It is not difficult to see why

Hôtel Biron and its grounds, Rue de Varenne, Paris, now the Musée Rodin.

Edith loved France. What she had always wanted, as a "priestess of the life of reason," was a society where ideas could be freely and continually exchanged, but where that exchange would be regulated by rules of good taste and good manners, in houses that were beautiful and at tables where the food was choice. Where else could such a society be found but in Paris? English society was as full of Philistines as American; German and Spanish were too stiff, Italian too indolent. But in France order was everywhere: in the châteaux, in the flower borders, in the design of the towns, above all in the thinking. Savants and scientists were to be found in the highest social circles. Streets were named after minor poets and sculptors.

Of course, there is a Paris for everybody. What Edith sought in the City of Light must have been very different from

what the "lost generation" sought in the 1920s. Everyone knows of the confrontation between Edith and the drunken Scott Fitzgerald when the latter, to shock her, announced that he and Zelda were living in a bordello. "What is a bordello, Mr. Fitzgerald?" Edith is reputed to have asked. No doubt she was mocking him. But the difference between the two novelists was

OPPOSITE: The young F. Scott Fitzgerald. ABOVE: Rue de Rivoli.

stated more seriously by Mrs. Chanler, who told me of a visit that Fitzgerald made to her in the Genesee Valley. He informed her that he had three ambitions, (1) to be faithful to his wife, (2) to write the best and clearest prose of the twentieth century, and (3) to become a close friend of Edith Wharton. Mrs. Chanler replied: "As to your first ambition, it is too personal for me to comment on. As to your second, I can only hope that you attain it. But as to your third, young man, I can promise you that, unless you cut down on your drinking, you're never going to be a friend of Edith Wharton's!"

111

World War I gave Edith the chance to show what she could do for France. Never for a moment did she see the war in any light but that of a struggle between civilization and barbarism, with France leading, as in a poster by Howard Chandler Christy, the forces of the enlightened. Across the Channel, Henry James struck the same note. Both were passionately sincere and ready to give all for the cause, but to modern, disillusioned ears the cry of embattled belligerents, particularly when they are behind the front and have no son there, sounds a bit shrill.

LEFT: World War I cartoon. OPPOSITE: Newbold Rhinelander.

Here is a fair sample of Edith on the war. She is writing
to her cousin, Tom Rhinelander, about his son Newbold who has
joined the ambulance corps in 1916:

> I am so glad you have given him this opportunity
> of seeing this great moment of history and lending a
> hand in the cause. I agree with you that such an ex-
> perience ought to last throughout life, and I am sure
> Newbold is the kind to make the most of it. I have
> been wondering why some of my able-bodied young
> cousins were not here taking a share in the struggle,
> and I am glad Newbold has shown the others the
> way.

Two of these "able-bodied young cousins," who preferred to wait until their own nation had become involved, were Frederic and LeRoy King, sons of Edith's first cousin, Ethel Rhinelander King. They ultimately redeemed themselves in Edith's eyes, and she modeled the hero of *The Marne* on LeRoy. Indeed, in later years, increasingly out of touch with the youth of her native land, Edith used the polished but anglicized language of

Edith and Walter Berry at the front.

the "King boys" as the model for her dialogue between young Americans. If people objected to a phrase as not in current American usage, she would simply reply: "The King boys use it."

In 1917, after the United States had finally entered the war, she wrote to a younger friend, Adele Burden:

> You must be having thrilling times, with both the boys in the war already. I would have given a great deal to have been in America during the last few

114

months, and I wish you could all have seen the reception of the first American regiment in Paris on the 4th of July and the gift of the American flag to General Pershing at the Invalides. It was really splendid, and the enthusiasm was tremendous.

Early in 1919 Thomas Rhinelander came abroad and found his son's grave. When he wrote Edith the final news, she replied:

> I had kept so irresistible a hope of seeing that dear young face again that your news was a shock to me— greater probably than to you, who had so wisely and admirably weighed the possibilities and refused to let yourself be deluded. But, after all, it is only right to call your journey "successful" and I am thankful indeed, that you know where he lies and that you received the blessed assurance that death was instantaneous for both and came before the fall. How few parents of aviators can say as much!

It may be wondered if Mrs. Burden felt much of a thrill at having "both the boys" in the war. Certainly Tom Rhinelander could not have, for in October of 1918, just before the Armistice, Newbold's plane was shot down behind enemy lines. It was three months before his family was officially notified of his death. In this terrible interim of doubt and desperate hope Edith showed herself at her best. She went to work with all her connections and all her efficiency to see what could be done to find out news of the young man. I have a series of letters showing how efficiently and vitally she worked on this. But I fear she may have struck a trivial note in mentioning her regret that there had not been time to do more for Newbold in literary circles:

> When I heard last summer that Newbold was in a camp near Clermont-Ferrand, I wrote at once to the Paul Bourgets, who were at Royat, to get in touch

America enters the war, Lorraine sector, October 1917.

General John J. Pershing.

New York parade, Fifth Avenue, New York.

War-torn Arras Cathedral.

with him, as I knew he would charm them and that
they would be kindness itself to him. And I knew
Bourget's talk would stimulate and interest him. Ar-
rangements were made *three times* for him to come
and lunch with them, but each time he was prevented,
and so the meeting never took place. I am so sorry,
for it would have been a joy on both sides, but his
camp was fifteen kilometers away and circulation is
not easy nowadays.

It is still a touching letter. It shows the dependence of
Edith's generation on well-organized, well-arranged, good,
proper things—all frustrated by the war. Right in the midst of
Armageddon, in all the horror, with the boy actually dead, there
is still the determination to have lunch with the Bourgets. One
may smile at it, but there is a kind of power and strength in it
nonetheless.

In her war work Edith showed an impressive, almost masculine power of organization and perseverance. Her writing was largely abandoned for the duration. One dares to speculate that some of the fury of her activity may have been an unconscious desire to make up to her murky gods for her abandonment of Teddy—and of America. She opened a workshop in Paris for women who had lost their jobs because of the war. She founded the American hostels which took care of 4500 French and Belgian refugees. She organized four little hospitals which took

OPPOSITE: Walter Berry and Edith with officer friend. BELOW: Hospital for Women and Children at Arromanches organized by Edith.

care of 440 tubercular patients. She established the Children of Flanders Rescue Committee which made itself responsible for 1000 young people. And, even more remarkably, she raised the money for all of these enterprises.

It was raised, as might have been expected, from her friends and relatives across the Atlantic. New York came to her aid. I have in my collection a copy of "Edith Wharton's War Charities in France," a report to the New York committee covering the

No 92   B.P.F

Reçu de Mrs Beverley Robinson
                                        la somme

de   cent quarante cinq francs cinquante centimes

MAISONS DE CONVALESCENCE
DES AMERICAN HOSTELS FOR REFUGEES

Paris   le 26 avril   1917.

E. Wharton

Receipt for a war contribution.

money raised and spent during the four years of the war, and listing the donations in cash and kind. Mrs. Cadwalader Jones had assumed the chairmanship of this committee and had made up a list of directors that reads like a blue book of New York society: Alexanders, Bishops, Cuttings, Delanos, Dodges, Morgans, Whitneys. It is perhaps not surprising that "Old New York" figured so strongly in the fiction that Edith wrote when she turned back to her principal occupation.

Armistice Day crowd in Paris.

But the war had taken its toll on noncombatants as well as on the fighters. Edith, no longer a young woman, was exhausted. When she went out on her balcony on the Rue de Varenne, on that November day of 1918, followed by all her household, to hear the bells of Paris ring in the Armistice, she may have felt, like France, that the victory had been too dearly purchased.

9

NOSTALGIA

She wanted now to live outside of Paris, and there had been many bargains in the northern suburbs in the dark spring of 1918. She had purchased the Pavillon Colombe, a charming, medium-sized eighteenth-century villa near the Forêt de Montmorency, originally built by two actresses. This "little house," as she wrote, always stood by her. It was perfect for the two pursuits that "never palled": writing and gardening. In April of 1918 she was almost ready to move in, and she wrote to Walter Maynard:

> I find myself a poor thing, and a week in Paris has convinced me of the need of another exile. My little funny house near Montmorency is nearly ready, and I hope in a few weeks to crawl into it, and spend a vegetable (but not vegetarian) summer. My doctor tells me I am "an elastic stretched too far, that will never tighten up again." This pretty symbol (which makes me feel as if I were perpetually slipping down my own ankles) presumably means that I must, in the horrid phrase, "be careful"—a need that usually presents itself just when one has pretty nearly ceased to care!

The aftermath of the war brought the wearisome business of obtaining the proper decorations for the American friends who had helped in the cause. Edith had solicited this help, and

Edith with her dogs. She described in *A Backward Glance* the "long ache of pity for animals" which nothing ever stilled in her.

Pavillon Colombe, St. Brice-sous-Forêt.

she had to see that the badges were given. But it was a sorry business to have to cadge for medals for the affluent middle-aged and elderly when her heart was full of the "young dead." She had to explain the delays and difficulties to Eunice Maynard, who had helped with her New York committee:

> Meanwhile, I am waiting for a propitious hour to ask for the Legion of Honour for Walter—for you will probably agree with me that he should have that or nothing. Mrs. Tyler and I both think that the opportunity will occur, for the government is under

Pavillon Colombe. Interior.

great obligations to our committee, and they know
it, and are very nice about it—but such a horde of
wire-pullers and notoriety hunters from our shores
have, alas, beset them with demands that I would
rather wait till they come forward spontaneously with
an offer, as I think they will.

You will ask me, in the meanwhile, how it is that
far less devoted and successful workers have received
all kinds of honours, and I can only say—I don't know!
But I suppose by nagging, grovelling, wire-pulling—
and bragging. (The latter certainly.) We have never
done any of these things, and if you saw the hungry

Pavillon Colombe

hordes at work you wouldn't want to be in any way
on a par with them! I think you will agree with all
this, but do send me a line if you do.

In the turmoil and dislocation of the postwar world Edith
began to look back with a new appreciation on the quiet, settled
New York of her childhood that she had once found so stultify-

126

Garden pond.

ing. If the older generation had spent their lives sweeping things under rugs, at least they had had rugs to sweep them under. And if the New York of the 1870s had disappeared as completely as Atlantis or the lowest layer of Schliemann's Troy, the very totality of its collapse seemed now to make it worth recalling in a vandal world that had only crude honesty, and often not that, to put in place of what it had destroyed. She confessed in her memoirs:

> When I was young it used to seem to me that the group in which I grew up was like an empty vessel into which no new wine would ever again be poured. Now I see that one of its uses lay in preserving a few drops of an old vintage too rare to be savored by a youthful palate.

It was in this mood of apology that she wrote *The Age of Innocence,* the finest of her novels. It is bathed in the same rich mood of nostalgia that permeates the chapters on her own childhood in *A Backward Glance,* a mood in which she tries to recapture a little girl's vision of the "mild blur of rosy and white-whiskered gentlemen, of ladies with bare sloping shoulders rising flower-like from voluminous skirts, peeped at from the stair-top while wraps were removed in the hall below." Time, however, had not blunted her sharp judgment of the personalities of that world. She still saw them as passive and confined. The only vigor shown by the male characters of *The Age of Innocence* is in their domination of the female. Mr. Welland is a querulous hypochondriac, with no opinions but many habits, and his wife has to find her fulfillment in being his slave. Sillerton Jackson brings to the study of scandal the science of a naturalist, and his sister spends her days collecting odd bits of gossip to round out his general picture. Mr. van der Luyden, through his obsequious consort and intermediary, rules society with the naïveté, simplicity, and pomposity of a true Victorian monarch. Even old Catherine Mingott, the ancestress and dowager, known to an awed New York as "Catherine the Great," is not, in the last analysis, so very formidable. Her bluster and independence are little more than poses, and in the big decisions she is swayed by her son and her lawyer.

But against the smallness and vapidity of its inhabitants the physical background of New York and Newport is painted with a richness of color and detail that delights the imagination. It is this constant contrast that makes the uniqueness of the novel. The old Academy of Music, with its shabby red-and-gold boxes, its carefully brushed, white-waistcoated, buttonhole-flowered gentlemen; the Julius Beauforts' conservatory, where camellias and tree ferns arch their foliage over seats of black-and-gold bamboo; May Archer's living room, with its little plush tables covered with silver toys and efflorescent photograph frames, the small bright lawns and big bright sea of Newport, succeed each other like colored slides to recall the dictum of Edmund Wilson about Edith being the pioneer and poet of interior decoration.

Such is the background from which Newland Archer springs. Like a Thackeray hero, he wears all the protective coloration of his times. He may be the best of his world, but the best, we feel, is none too good. He is burstingly complacent, delighted with his own fine, vigorous youth, with his promising but not taxing law practice, with the adoration of his widowed mother and old-maid sister, and the love of his beautiful but unimaginative fiancée. He is equally delighted with his own taste for books and his eye for pictures; he prides himself on his ability to talk with artists and writers in the Century Club as well as to hold his own with the aristocratic young bloods at the Knickerbocker. And he is delighted, too, that he has sowed his wild oats, that a desultory affair with a married woman has prepared him to cope with his future bride's assumed ignorance in all matters of sex. Newland Archer, in short, is about as fatuous a young man as one could conceive of, the roundest possible peg in the roundest possible hole.

Yet everything might have been all right for him had it not been for the arrival of Ellen Olenska, the beautiful, disenchanted cousin of his fiancée, who had fled home from a titled Polish brute of a husband. Ellen sees the New York

OVERLEAF: Walter Berry and Edith viewing war damage.

society that to Archer is brilliant, glittering, even formidable, as a quaint, innocent refuge from the black storms of her European life. "I'm sure I'm dead and buried, and this dear old place is heaven," she tells him on their first meeting as she gazes about at the boxes of the Academy of Music. It is of the essence of Edith's plan that only the gentle pinprick of Ellen's half-intended sarcasm is needed to burst the overblown balloon of Archer's self-satisfaction. Indeed, so insecure are the walls of the society which has produced him that they tremble before the first puff of an irreverent breath. For the rebellion of Ellen Olenska, in the last analysis, boils down to little more than that she has brought home with her a bit of the sophisticated simplicity of an older civilization. It is symbolized, like everything else, by the decoration of her drawing room, with its "small, slender tables of dark wood, a delicate little Greek bronze on the chimney-piece, and a stretch of red damask nailed on the discolored wallpaper behind a couple of Italian-looking pictures in old frames."

Her effect on Archer is immediate and catastrophic. Not only does he learn about love; he learns that his whole life has been premised on a false hypothesis. His discovery of himself and re-evaluation of his household gods form the principal topic of a story which is one of the very few in which Edith confined herself to a single point of view. In this respect it resembles James's *The Ambassadors*, where we follow the re-education of Lambert Strether entirely in Strether's mind. Edith, however, deviates from the strictness of James's method in that she peers over Archer's shoulder to point out aspects of the New York scene that his imagination is too limited to encompass. This is necessary because Archer, before he has developed into the sensitive and likable man of the later chapters, is too egregious an ass to be able to tell us anything really significant about the society that he uncritically admires. Paris stretches Strether's imagination without in the least altering his character, but Ellen

Edith and her maid, Gross.

Oaklawn, the Charles H. Russell house in Newport, R.I., one of the sites of the archery contests. The chocolate color, the striped veranda roof, the spiky green plants, suggest that, in combination with the August Belmont house, it may have served as a model for Julius Beaufort's summer home in *The Age of Innocence*.

Olenska turns Newland Archer from a stuffed shirt into a man.

Archer's emancipation ultimately carries him too far, for in the end he is ready to ditch his wife, tear himself up by the roots, and flee to Europe in search of Ellen, and May can hold him only by the time-honored expedient of announcing her pregnancy. He is thus trapped for life in a New York routine, the satisfactions of which have been permanently soured. Yet neither he nor Ellen nor their creator regard the sacrifice as a sterile one. Had he followed Ellen to Europe, *The Age of Innocence* might have become *Anna Karenina*, and Ellen might have ended as badly as Tolstoi's heroine. The only way that she and Archer can convert their love into a thing of beauty is by renunciation. And the twist of the plot is that the value of renunciation has been taught them not, after all, by the wise old civilization of Europe, but by the very society of brownstone New York that they have both so resented. Ellen tells Archer:

> "It was you who made me understand that under the dullness there are things so fine and sensitive and delicate that even those I most cared for in my other life look cheap in comparison. I don't know how to explain myself, but it seems as if I'd never before understood with how much that is hard and shabby and base the most exquisite pleasures may be paid."

The balance of Archer's moderately civic and uneventful life is covered in a couple of pages. In addition to being a conscientious if undemonstrative husband and father, he serves a term in the State Assembly, fails of re-election, and drops thankfully back to obscure if useful municipal work and from that to the writing of occasional articles in reforming weeklies. His own career is summed up as follows:

> It was little enough to look back on; but when he remembered to what the young men of his gen-

eration and his set had looked forward—the narrow groove of money-making, sport, and society to which their vision had been limited—even his small contribution to the new state of things seemed to count, as each brick counts in a well-built wall. He had done little in public life—he would always be by nature a contemplative and a dilettante—but he had had high things to contemplate, great things to delight in; and one great man's friendship to be his strength and pride.

The great man, as we have seen before, is Theodore Roosevelt. Edith does not explain how *he* was able to transcend the limitations of that brownstone world. But no doubt the Rough Rider would have proved an exception to any rule, and rules

Theodore Roosevelt, whom Edith invoked as "O great American" in her memorial poem *Within the Tide*. She entertained for him on his visit to Paris in 1910.

are what the novelist is interested in. Being herself an exception, or at least a refugee (for she had little of the rebel in her), she could never quite conceal a faint condescension for the victims of old New York. The thing that she keeps stressing about the Archers and Wellands and Jacksons and Mingotts is that, however dear and good and honorable they may be, they are not really alive. They have missed, like Newland Archer, the flower of life. But, having missed it—and one feels sure that Edith believed that most people, everywhere, *did* miss it—they conducted their lives with a commendable dignity and style. What more, she seems to ask, could one really expect of them? Archer reveals his credo, which was probably the author's, when he thinks back on his life with May:

> Their long years together had shown him that it did not so much matter if marriage was a dull duty, as long as it kept the dignity of a duty: lapsing from that, it became a mere battle of ugly appetites. Looking about him, he honored his own past and mourned for it. After all, there was good in the old ways.

It remains to be asked: *were* they that way? Was the society of that old New York as lacking in imagination and adventure as Edith makes out? Was it as bound by petty precepts and precedents? The diary of George Templeton Strong, first published in 1952, bears evidence that it was. Strong was a member of that society and on visiting terms with Edith's parents. He kept a voluminous and fascinating journal that covers his life in New York from 1835, when he was a student at Columbia, to his death forty years later. He belonged to the generation before Newland Archer, but if Edith had chosen to cast her novel in the form of a journal, it could well have been a duplicate. Strong's public career was perhaps more important than Archer's (he was on Lincoln's Sanitary Commission during the war), and there is no hint that his marriage was ever troubled by an Ellen Olenska, but the entries give us the same picture of a conscientious and honorable man, somewhat lacking in force, with much enthusiasm but less taste in artistic matters, a dutiful member of charitable boards, a lawyer with a leisurely practice, kindly, observant, prejudiced, sharp, and very bitter indeed at the double tide of new money and immigration that was swamping his Knickerbocker New York. "These be thy Gods, O Israel!" he exclaimed in derision before the newly unveiled frock-coated bronze statue of Commodore Vanderbilt. There is a section of the diary, not included in the 1952 edition, where he describes a crisis in his cousin Charley Strong's marriage and how the tight little society of that day drew itself together around the vacillating wife and ejected her would-be lover from the city. It is strikingly reminiscent of Edith's description of the farewell dinner party which the Newland Archers give for Ellen Olenska, where Archer at last realizes, from their very silence on the subject, that all his relatives and friends have assumed that he is having an affair with the guest of honor. The united tribe is irresistible—at least to its own members.

10

THE 1920s

The Age of Innocence received the Pulitzer Prize in 1921, but this honor was spoiled for Edith by her discovery that her novel had been used by the committee as a handy substitute to keep the prize away from Sinclair Lewis's *Main Street*. Prizes were not, on the whole, a happy chapter in her life. A few years later her friends Robert and Mildred Bliss rather humiliatingly failed in an all-out effort to obtain for her the Nobel Prize, as she herself, in 1913, had failed to obtain it for Henry James. In *Hudson River Bracketed* she bitterly and perhaps a bit crudely satirized the politics of prize-giving, naming the character who is the widow of the award giver Mrs. Pulsifer. Lewis, in any case, did not hold his missed prize against Edith, for he subsequently dedicated *Babbitt* to her.

Public honors continued to flow. In the spring of 1923 she crossed the Atlantic to receive a Doctorate of Letters from Yale University. Her trip was a brief one, but she visited the Maynards on Long Island in the beautiful little French château that Ogden Codman had designed for them in Jericho. Edith was enchanted to find that these friends had created on their side of the Atlantic the same French atmosphere that she had gone abroad to seek. Staying in Islip with Olivia Cutting, on the other hand, she found echoes not of her current but of her old

The Walter Maynard house at Jericho, Long Island, N.Y., designed by Ogden Codman, where Edith stayed on her last visit to the United States.

Ste. Claire-le-Chateau,

life, and she returned for one evening to the New York of her childhood. Olivia Cutting's granddaughter, Iris Origo, described this for an English paper. She related how Edith refused to be led into any discussions of persons or events in France—of Carlo Placi or Madame de Noailles—and how at each such attempt she gently and firmly steered the conversation back to old friends and old memories of New York:

> The W's house on 11th Street, had it really been pulled down? Did her hostess remember the night they had dined there before the Colony Club ball? The X's daughter, the fair one, had she married her young Bostonian? Had Z indeed lost all his money? For the whole evening this mood continued. At one moment only—as, the last guest gone, she turned half-way up the stairs to wave good-night—I caught a glimpse of the other Edith, elegant, formidable, as hard and dry as porcelain. Then, as she looked down

Hyères, ramparts, and gardens.

on her old friends, the face softened, even the erectness of her spine relaxed a little. She was no longer the trim, hard European hostess, but a nice old American lady. Edith had come home.

But not to stay: It was her last visit to her native land. With the war behind her and the past recaptured, with a Pulitzer Prize and a Yale doctorate to her credit, Edith now settled down to the routine that would last till her death. Winters were spent in a converted monastery on the Riviera, Ste. Claire-le-Château, a long, low stone edifice with a crenelated roof and a wide sunny terrace overlooking the town of Hyères and the sparkling Mediterranean. For the summers she had the exquisite Pavillon Colombe, just north of Paris, whose rooms she filled with beautiful things and whose grounds she embellished with a rose garden and apple orchard. Besides the many gardeners in both these places who were required to keep up the perfect plots, there

was the faithful corps of old retainers, experts in ministering to their mistress's comfort: White, the English butler, Cook, the American chauffeur, Gross, the Alsatian, and Elise, the French, maid. Edith's relationship with her servants was always close. She approached housework with them as a team. Once tried and proved, they became members of her family, to be cherished and petted. This was in marked distinction to her treatment of the staff of hotels. The latter had *not* been proved; they were part of the outside and potentially hostile world. It was the same distinction, basically, that she made with all people. Edith lived in a spiritual fortress. Once admitted, friends and servants were treated to the same possessive loyalty. She even kept track of old retainers of her long-deceased parents to make sure that they were never in need.

All observers agree that Edith carried her household duties into the realm of art. There was something almost relentless in her perfectionism. Everything in both houses, whether it was the placing of a chair, the hanging of a picture, or the ordering of a meal, was the subject of her personal supervision. She was able to accomplish her writing in the early morning when her house guests were hardly conscious of it. By eleven o'clock she was ready for the day, which included, in addition to the organization of the household and the preparation of the events of her social life, all sorts of interesting and exciting excursions. She loved to have guests, but it was necessary that they fit in with the plan of the day. At one point she seriously jeopardized her friendship with the great art critic, Bernard Berenson, by objecting petulantly to his habit of taking a nap after lunch, which she regarded as a waste of time.

Then there were the trips, every year—the indefatigable

OPPOSITE: Two faithful servants: Charles Cook, Edith's chauffeur, and Gross, her maid. BELOW: Edith with Robert Norton. "If there is one thing on which she prides herself it is her unerring eye for a picnic-place." Percy Lubbock, *Portrait of Edith Wharton*.

sight-seeing. This letter to Mrs. Chanler, in 1925, conveys some sense of Edith's breathless rush in pursuit of beauty and culture:

> Well, now to other fields: fields of wild flowers in the Pyrenees, so inconceivably beautiful and rare that they still fill my inward eye. I had ten days of wonderful motoring with Robert [Robert Norton] and vaguely remember sending you a postcard. We saw Agde (very fine—I did not know it), the great Cistercian Abbey of Fontfroide, the splendid brick

The Vallée du Lys

church of Pamiers, the exquisite cloister of St. Lizier (close by) and then we plunged into the Pyrenees at Luchon and wandered among flowers and Romanesque churches—little *"frustes"* among the hills; and even dipped for one long, dazzled day into Spain, motoring to the very end of the Val d'Aran which, in its singular spring purity, all narcissus and gentian and golden poplars and flowering fruit trees and cold rushing rivulets, was so like Keats's "Eve of St. Mark" that my heart trembled. . . . Like all honest letter

near Luchon, Pyrenees.

writers I have begun by talking about myself and, having emptied my sack, have no time to turn my attention to yours, which was a real horn of plenty. I am so glad that London was such a success and that you got hold of the right people and saw the perfect things.

It was an expensive life, and Edith was not the heiress that some of her friends supposed. When she died in 1937, the two trusts of which she was income beneficiary under her father's and mother's wills totaled less than $700,000, and the securities that she owned outright amounted to only $125,000. Even though these sums may have been larger before 1929, they would probably not have thrown off an income adequate to a style of living (what Percy Lubbock called Edith's "state") that required two large places and nineteen employees. Edith, in these years, must have written for Mammon as well as art. She learned to make good use of all the popular media: the pictorial magazine, the stage, ultimately the movies. When D. Appleton & Co. offered her a bigger advance than Scribner's, she promptly deserted her old publisher. Charles Scribner was later to describe this as the greatest blow that his pride as a publisher ever received.

There is an inconsistency between some of the pictures of Edith in her middle years that can be reconciled if one bears in mind the bias of the different observers. Henry James and Percy Lubbock are decidedly literary in their descriptions of her. They saw their friend in terms of high adventure and in all the perfection of her accomplishments, literary, architectural, horticultural. To James she was "our great Edith," whirled around by the finest silver strings, half-bird, half-angel. She swooped down on her poor worms of friends with a flash of iridescent wings and dazzled them with her ravaging and devouring energy. Her only fault was that she exposed worms to "worm-like consciousness." It is easy to detect behind such hyperbole the discomfort of the set old bachelor interrupted in his labors and to deduce that he found Edith "bossy." But the image of the boss is always tempered by the image of the soaring flight. If Edith was "an angel of devastation," she was still an angel.

But there is nothing angelic or eagle-like in the first impression of Nicky Mariano, Berenson's friend and companion; "she described" Edith as "a conventionally dressed woman, jerky in her movements, somehow ill at ease, with an ugly mouth, shaped like a savings box." Nor is Consuelo Balsan much more complimentary: "In appearance she had the precise primness of an old maid—there was something puritanical about her in spite of the cosmopolitan, rather Bohemian life she affected." The ladies were not encumbered by gallantry.

Nicky Mariano, despite Edith's mouth, ultimately became her friend and somewhat qualified admirer. It is significant that she broke through the novelist's reserve by making a polite inquiry about her maid Elise, again evidence of Edith's attractive devotion to dependents. Miss Mariano now passed over the drawbridge into the inner Wharton court where there was much enchantment in bright talk and laughter for the guest who was willing to submit to the whims and planning of his conscientious yet arbitrary hostess. But woe to the intruder! "The change in her if anybody from the outside world turned up was almost unbelievable. From being simple, gay, ready to tease her friends and to let herself be teased by them, she became stiff, conventional, almost frozen up, and created an atmosphere of *gêne* all around her."

I have already spoken of the epicene quality of Edith's "court." She wanted men to be men, and yet she didn't. It was the same with the heroes of her novels. She had something in common with James's fierce little suffragette in *The Bostonians*, Olive Chancellor, who scorned the support of males, saying that no man who cared about women's rights could be a real man.

Nicky Mariano pictures Edith at her happiest, in 1927, at sixty-five, seated in bed in an elegant wrapper with a coquettish lace cap, her writing things all about her, with her Pekingese dogs at her feet and Walter Berry seated nearby, making the morning plans for her guests and household. Indeed, the coquette was always lurking behind the splendid chatelaine. The young Gabrielle Chanler, one of Mrs. Chanler's daughters, who introduced her hostess to a game of spotting traits of character by noting words uttered in free association, pointed out that all of Edith's tested words referred to men or clothes. "Youth, youth, you are so cruel," her hostess reproached her.

With men, with friends, with philosophy, even with religion, she had a way of pulling herself up short. I do not mean to imply by this that she never had a love affair, but that she shunned the depths of intimacy in friendship as she shunned them in philosophical inquiry into the ultimate meaning of life. She kept her citadel guarded from the too-probing heart as well as from the too-probing mind. She liked to know precisely what she was dealing with.

The intimates all speak of her habitual reserve. Mrs. Chanler told me that whenever anyone kissed Edith—an old friend or relation—she would raise a hand to the person's shoulder as if instinctively to guard herself against any bestial inclination that might erupt. Charles DuBos, the sympathetic young Frenchman who translated *The House of Mirth*, wrote that in thirty years of close friendship he had had only one moment of true intimacy with Edith, when, in the course of an afternoon's motor excursion to an old church and a discussion of love and marriage in the poetry of Browning, she had suddenly spoken out passionately about the poverty, the "miserable poverty" of any love outside of wedlock. DuBos had thought that this might be the prelude to a freer exchange in their future conversations, but, to his disappointment, the very reverse had been true. Edith had no doubt been as shocked as he had been surprised by her unwonted outburst. She must have seen no gain for either in such lapses.

The hardest thing to convey in any picture of Edith in the last twenty years of her life is the sense of what a wonderful woman she must have been, and how delightful and warm a companion. Laura White, the eldest of Mrs. Chanler's daughters, complained to me once that Edith is constantly shown in memoirs as stiff, reserved, and formal, as too exclusively the great lady of letters. That, of course, was one side of her. But what is much less usually stressed is her gaiety, her buoyancy, her laughter, her love of life. It is all these in Percy Lubbock's beautiful book, which is certainly the best thing that has been written about her. Perhaps some tiny sense of how she could be with her intimates is conveyed by a little Christmas poem that she addressed to Laura White and her husband Larry and their family of seven children. It was soon to be eight. Edith places the fecundity of the Whites in charming contrast to her own lack of it:

> Goldfish, four pekes, a poodle, and a flock
> Of fantail pigeons roosting in the rock—
> For mothering these no Montyon prize is given;
> Yet, enviable parents of the seven,
> Some merit to the humble task ascribe,
> And from Ste. Claire's furred, finned, and feathered
>   tribe
> Receive a greeting sent across the sea
> To howsoever many Whites there be.

Robert and Mildred Bliss had become friends of Edith's during the First World War when Robert Bliss was stationed in the American Embassy in Paris. In those more leisurely days of diplomacy America's representatives abroad had a good deal of time to pursue their own intellectual interests, and the Blisses had many of these and a great fortune to implement them. They

Terrace of Ste. Claire-le-Chateau, Hyères.

Goldfish, four Pekes, a Poodle, & a flock
Of fan-Tail Pigeons roosting in the rock —
For mothering these no Montyon Prize is given;
Yet, enviable parents of the Seven,
Some merit to their humble Task ascribe,
And from Ste Claire's furred, finned & feathered tribe
Receive a greeting sent across the Sea
To how so ever many Whites there be.

                          Edith

          Ste Claire-le-Château
                Xmas 1928

A Christmas card with greetings to Lawrence and Laura Chanler White.

ultimately concentrated on the art and history of the Byzantine Empire and founded the Byzantine Institute at Dumbarton Oaks in the District of Columbia which is now administered by Harvard. In 1926 Robert Bliss was appointed American Minister to Sweden, and it was while he was stationed there that he and his wife conceived the idea of obtaining the Nobel Prize for Edith.

She was aboard the yacht *Osprey*, which she had chartered for a cruise with friends in the Mediterranean. She wrote to Mildred Bliss from the ship:

> The yacht is simply perfect. I should like to go off in her for two months every year, so you know what will happen to the Nobel Prize if *I* get it!! I am embarrassed by your questions, though so touched by your thought, for I don't know what being "sponsored" consists in. I am Hon. Litt. Doc. of Yale (the only woman so honored, as far as I know) and Gold Medallist of The American Society of Arts and Letters—again the only woman, or at least it was so two years ago, when I received the medal. It seems to me—quite frankly—that the American men of letters who should long since have got the prize, are only two, and both dead: Henry James and the great historian Henry C. Lea. I moved heaven and earth to

get it for Henry, but the Scandinavians had never heard of him!!! Of the living, I see only W. C. Brownell, the critic. As I understand it, the prize is meant to crown a career, not to encourage a debut. You are a dear to have thought of me and I shall always feel that a little fraction of the prize is mine —your share in it—whoever gets the whole.

Edith continued to be humorous about the prize in her correspondence with the Blisses, but she nevertheless busied herself about forwarding copies of her books and obtaining the necessary letters of endorsement. She even went so far as to arrange that one of her sponsors, Paul Bourget, should be "put

OPPOSITE: The yacht *Osprey*, chartered by Edith in 1926. She toyed with the idea of paying for this Mediterranean cruise by writing an account of it to be called *The Sapphire Way*. BELOW: The yachting party: Henry Spencer (a last-minute substitute), Robert Norton, Edith, Margaret Chanler (Mrs. Winthrop Chanler), and Logan Pearsall Smith.

wise" so that he would "know in what terms to sing my praises to the Nobels!" All of the Blisses' good efforts, including their sending to the Nobel Committee a letter of recommendation from Chief Justice William Howard Taft (a curious choice) came to no avail, and, in January of 1928, Robert Bliss was obliged to cable Edith that the prize had gone elsewhere. It is most mortifying to miss an honor that one has shown a desire to obtain, but Edith wrote at once to Mildred Bliss this sensible and dignified letter:

> I was really touched that you and Robert should have taken the trouble to cable me about the Nobel Prize. I never had the least expectation of getting it in 1926, '27 or any other year, as far as the eye can reach, and I accepted your friendly suggestion to *poser ma candidature* only because it came from you and never with any idea of even *your* achieving any result. The giving of the last prize to Grazia Deledda, when artists like Serao and DiRoberto went to the grave without it—d'Annunzio is still there to receive it—shows, alas, the uselessness of attempting to award such prizes with any degree of justice or even approximate insight. But do believe, both of you, that I'm nonetheless touched by your trying to pull off the crown for me, where Henry James and Hardy did not get it.

In 1928 she lost the friend of her lifetime, Walter Berry, and she took the loss hard. One cannot help finding, however, in her correspondence a certain satisfaction that she was able so completely to dominate the deathbed. I have heard people say that Edith suffered in the last years of Berry's life from his coldness and neglect. I have even heard it suggested that he gave to other ladies the same kind of intimate friendship that he had shared with Edith. I do not imply by this that he was having love affairs. He was an old man, and, anyway, he had never had a great reputation in that field. Lady Ribblesdale told me that it was said in Paris that, unlike some gentleman callers who left their hostess with a baby, Berry left them with a book.

Walter Berry.

I think it more likely that his seeming neglect of Edith came from his absorption with just the kind of young people that she found least sympathetic: the "lost" generation represented by his wild young cousin Harry Crosby who founded the Black Sun Press in Paris. Berry loved to play the role of the grand old survival of another era at the Crosby parties. But if there was in fact any coolness on his part toward Edith at the end, she must, by taking charge of his sickbed, have had the gratification of rectifying the immediate past and saving her memory of a perfect friendship.

Berry had an operation for appendicitis in 1927, after which he spent two weeks of convalescence with Edith at Hyères. When he returned to Paris, he plunged straight back into his varied round of business, law, charities, and society, and soon suffered a stroke. When Edith hurried north to see him, she found him able to speak clearly and without a trace of paralysis, but weak and shattered. She proceeded to take over the reins of his life and to write to his friends and clients.

He seemed to get better, and in November he was well enough to tell Edith that he would come out to lunch with her at the Pavillon Colombe. He did not arrive, and she received the message that he had had a second stroke. He was ill nine days, speechless but lucid. Immediately after his death she wrote to Mildred Bliss:

> Think! I was twenty-one when we first met and his mind was clear to the end, and he remembered it all. He was paralysed on Oct. 2 and for two days would see no one. I was in the background, of course, but the doctors said the only hope was to do just as he wished in every way, and I knew the reason. He thought I would get the doctors to prolong his life in the dreadful new ways they have. At last he asked for me, and as soon as I went into the room I said: 'I will never let anyone do anything to prolong your

life.' He took my hand then, and we had the last four days together. He could not speak, but I said over names and asked everything I could think of, and he always sighed "No," so I just stayed alone with him. It is almost more than the common run of human sorrow, but then he was so much more than other people.

Two weeks later she wrote again to Mildred Bliss. She seemed to be trying to console herself with the memory that, at the end at least, she had been everything to Berry:

> I am sure I told you that I was all alone with him through it all, that he refused to let anyone else be sent for, though I repeated the names of various friends I thought he might want to see, and that through the unspeakable tragedy of it all I had at least the comfort of knowing that he understood everything I said and that his thoughts travelled back with mine over our long, long friendship. That is the only memory that I can bear to dwell on now, for the sight of that imprisoned, agonized mind, pleading for expression out of his poor vivid eyes, would be too cruel otherwise—is too cruel still, at times. I don't know which of Walter's possessions, if any, will be sold, but he left me the pictures I liked best, and all his library. . . .

According to Caresse Crosby, wife of Harry Crosby, Berry's cousin and residuary legatee, the will left Edith not *all* his library, but only such of it as she should select. Legally, however, this would have entitled Edith to all of it, and evidently this was the position she took, for Caresse recorded that she and Harry had to fight hard to resist the "grab act." Edith was undoubtedly burningly sincere in her scornful belief that the relatives who took possession of Berry's effects had little in common with the great deceased. She wrote to Alice Garrett:

Edith, Pavillon Colombe.

It is all a desert ahead, but I hope it will seem less arid when I get out of all these matters, and can go back quietly to the thought of the incomparable being he was. At present, seeing all the little people crawling over him nearly kills me.

11

FAMILY

Edith always kept up carefully with her many Rhinelander and Jones cousins, but family for her in the postwar years consisted mostly of her niece, Beatrix Jones Farrand, and Beatrix's mother, Mary Cadwalader Jones. The latter was not, strictly speaking, Edith's sister-in-law, having been divorced from her brother, Frederic Jones, but in spite of this she remained to all intents and purposes a true sister until her death at the age of eighty-four, only two years before Edith's own. Mary Jones, or Minnie as she was called, occupied a small house on 11th Street in Manhattan and was famous for her Sunday lunches. She had an outgiving, lovable personality, irradiating those charms of intellect and humor that make a hostess an unforgettable figure. She would have laughed at the idea that she presided over a salon, but that was precisely what she did. Her intimate friends included Henry James, Henry and Brooks Adams, Marion Crawford, and Theodore Roosevelt. Her financial means were limited, and she was assisted through the years by her sister-in-law who employed her as a literary agent to handle some of her publishing problems in New York. But helping Minnie Jones, other than on a business basis, was not always an easy thing, and Edith had to work through her niece, Beatrix, to attain the necessary results. Here, in 1922, is an

Edith with an unidentified friend.

example of Edith's methods. She is writing Beatrix to arrange for a motorcar for her mother:

> After I had thought of the motor plan someone told me that in New York it wasn't much use, as the circulation was so congested that it was much better to take taxis as required; but I knew that your mother *wouldn't* take taxis if I arranged any vague plan of that kind! And now your letter shows that you quite agree with me in thinking that the motor will relieve her of worry and fatigue and give her an easier winter, and I am too delighted to be able to do it and hope that your sojourn in town will be made easier too in sharing the chariot with her. At any rate she will certainly *voiturer* all her lame ducks, and I hope Elizabeth has found a chauffeur with a large family so that pretexts for generosity will not be wanting. I rely on you also to see that she gets a comfortable car and careful driver rather than to try to screw down a hundred dollars or so a month. I'm quite "game" for the $1,600, and may it be a success! It makes me chuckle to think that this very morning the chauffeur is calling for orders.

Beatrix Farrand, Minnie's only child, was Edith's only niece and, as she died childless, there are no living descendants of Edith's parents. Those who feel that Edith's talents must have come from some bloodstrain more exotic than is to be found in the Jones and Rhinelander family trees should consider the talents of Beatrix. She became a famous landscape architect and designed the great gardens at Dumbarton Oaks in Washington, D. C., for Robert and Mildred Bliss. One of the rare occasions when Edith acknowledged the gratification of her own accomplishments was when she congratulated Beatrix on obtaining a commission from Yale:

> It's a great satisfaction, isn't it, to find one's work recognized, and know that the dedicated sense one

ABOVE: Garden pool, Dumbarton Oaks. BELOW: The rose garden, where Robert and Mildred Bliss were interred.

had within one corresponds to an outward reality? I know the feeling, and am sure you'll agree with me that it's about the best there is in this world of uncertainties. I'm very proud of your success, and perhaps in my pride there is more understanding of what it means than if I hadn't my own trade to measure your achievement by.

There was, however, one still closer relative, who also lived in Paris. Edith's brother Harry, after a long, idle existence of mild dissipation, had finally married a woman with whom she would have nothing to do. Her attitude toward this unfortunate brother represents the other side of the coin of her human charity. When people played the game by her rules she was loyal to the end, but when they violated what she regarded as basic responsibilities, she could be very unforgiving. Harry died in 1922, and Edith attended his funeral but did no more. She described it to her niece Beatrix in these terms:

> Will you please give your mother my love. . . . I seem in writing to her the last time not to have said anything about Harry's funeral. My silence was not intentional. But really, the ghastly thing once over, I swept it all out of my mind. Susie Gray and Walter Berry very kindly went with me, and we sat in the front pew on the opposite side of the aisle from the Bereaved One. The church was full—I can't think who the people were—and the coffin covered with a pall of wired carnations. After the funeral the verger asked if I would assist at the *défilé* in the sacristy with *Madame* Jones, and I said '*Merci, non.*' The widow was then led sobbing from the scene, and we walked out of the church before the people left their seats, so that the few Americans who were there—Nelson Winthrop, Herrick Riggs, I don't remember who else —saw that I was present, which was what I wanted. Then *that* book closed for me.

THE
GLIMPSES
of the MOON
EDITH WHARTON

12

THE LAST BOOKS

As long as Edith had elected, after the war, to continue
writing about the social life of a New York that she had given
up even visiting, she would have done better to restrict herself
to those eras with which she had been personally familiar. The
four perfect little stories that make up *Old New York* evoke
the atmosphere of the last century quite as brilliantly as any
parts of *The Age of Innocence*. But she was too concerned
with the world around her to write only of the past. She wanted
to interpret the age in which she lived and to seek out the origin
and cause of the increasing number of things in it that angered
her. She wrote to Eunice Maynard in 1923 that she would have
to come "frisking over to see the new United States which I
badly need to do if I'm to go on writing about it." Henry James
had warned Minnie Jones as far back as 1902 that Edith should
be "tethered in native pastures" even if it reduced her to "a
backyard in New York." But, alas, she neglected both the
warning of the master and her own intuition.

The Glimpses of the Moon (1922) was first serialized in
Pictorial Review, which may give the clue to the author's lapse
of style and taste. The mawkish jacket of the book which de-

ABOVE AND OPPOSITE: Edith with Eunice Maynard (Mrs. Walter Maynard) in the garden at Pavillon Colombe.

picts an Italian villa on Lake Como by moonlight makes the reader rub his eyes and look again to be sure that he is dealing with Edith Wharton. Nick and Susy Lansing, two bright young penniless hangers-on of the international set, have married on the understanding that their bond may be dissolved at the option of the first to find a richer spouse. Nick is again the dilettante hero, but now, for the first time, reader and author see him from radically different points of view. To the reader he is, quite simply, an unmitigated cad, perfectly content to live in the borrowed houses of rich friends so long as his wife agrees not to steal the cigars or to take any overt part in the blind-folding of their hostesses' deceived husbands. On these two commandments hang all his law and his prophets, and when Susy has violated both (in each case, for his sake), he abruptly abandons her to pursue an heiress. It is impossible to imagine how Edith could have picked such a man as the hero of a

romance unless she seriously believed that he represented what a gentleman had sunk to in the seventeen years that had elapsed since the publication of *The House of Mirth*. But could even Lawrence Selden have degenerated to a Nick Lansing? And could Lily Bart ever have stolen cigars? Surely the world had not been entirely taken over by the Lansings and their dismal set of international drifters who blur together in a maze of furs and jewels and yachts. Edith's preoccupation with vulgarity had for the moment vulgarized her perceptions.

With the publication of *The Mother's Recompense* in 1925, reviewers began to note this drop in quality of Edith's fiction, and she minded it all the more keenly in that she may have sensed the basis for it. She wrote to Mrs. Chanler:

> Thank you ever so fondly for taking the trouble to tell me why you like my book. Your liking it would be a great joy, but to know why is a subtle consolation for densities of incomprehension which were really beginning to discourage me. No one else

171

has noticed "Desolation is a delicate thing" [the quotation on the title page] or understood that the key is there. The title causes great perplexity, but several reviewers think it means that the mother was "recompensed" by "the love of an honest man." One enthusiast thinks it has lifted me to the same height as Galsworthy, another that I am now equal to Scott Fitzgerald. And the *Saturday Review of American [Literature]* critic says I have missed my chance because the book "ought to have ended tragically." *Ought to!* You will wonder that the priestess of the life of reason should take such things to heart, and I wonder too. I never have minded before, but as my work reaches its close, I feel so sure that it is either nothing or far more than they know. And I wonder a little desolately which.

The caricature of American life in the later novels becomes grotesque. The towns are given names like Delos, Aeschylus, Lohengrin, or Halleluja, and the characters speak an anglicized dialect (derived from the "King boys"?) full of such terms as "Hang it!" "Chuck it!" "He's a jolly chap," and "A fellow needs. . . ." The town slogan of Euphoria in *Hudson River Bracketed* is "Me for the front row." And the American face! How it haunts Edith! It is "as unexpressive as a football"; it might have been made by "a manufacturer of sporting goods." Its sameness encompasses her "with its innocent uniformity." How many of such faces would it take "to make up a single individuality"? And, ironically enough, as her indignation mounts, her style loses its old precision and begins to take on the slickness of a popular magazine story. Compare, for example, these two descriptions of a lady on the threshold of a European hotel. The first is from *Madame de Treymes*, written in 1907, one of her Jamesian passages, highly polished:

> The mere fact of her having forgotten to draw
> on her gloves as they were descending in the hotel

Margaret Chanler, her daughter, Laura, and
Prince Camillo Borghese at a Roman Meet.

173

lift from his mother's drawing room was, in this con-
nection, charged with significance to Durham. She
was the kind of woman who always presents herself
to the mind's eye as completely equipped, as made
of exquisitely cared for and finely related details; and
that the heat of her parting with his family should
have left her unconscious that she was emerging glove-
less into Paris seemed, on the whole, to speak hope-
fully for Durham's future opinion of the city. Even
now, he could detect a certain confusion, a desire to
draw breath and catch up with her life, in the way
she dawdled over the last buttons in the dimness of
the porte-cochère, while her footman, outside, hung
on her retarded signal.

The second is from *The Glimpses of the Moon*, fifteen
years later:

> But on the threshold a still more familiar figure
> met her: that of a lady in exaggerated pearls and
> sables, descending from an exaggerated motor, like
> the motors in magazine advertisements, the huge arks
> in which jeweled beauties and slender youths pause
> to gaze at snow peaks from an Alpine summit.

Specimens of old New York in the novels now become
spindly and ridiculous, like Mr. Wyant in *Twilight Sleep* and
Mr. Spears in *Hudson River Bracketed*. The Wheaters in *The
Children* are meant to be rich New Yorkers traveling in Europe.
Their children, of various nationalities, their absurd marital
mix-up, their impossible, red-carpeted, be-yachted life, with a
movie star ex-wife whose favorite swear word is "Fudge!" and
an American-born princess who hopes that the size of families
will be regulated by legislation, constitute a crude parody of
international drifters. Edith has no true insight into their lives;
she stands apart like her spokesman, Mrs. Sellars, in disdain,
describing the Wheaters only in terms of snobbish and disap-
proving suppositions.

174

Better things, however, were in store. It is fascinating to note that the character who now emerged from Edith's imagination to restore the failing energy of her fiction is a man, a fullblooded man, Vance Weston, the hero of *Hudson River Bracketed* and the first such hero of all her novels and tales. Why did he have to wait until her sixty-seventh year and be born in an American Midwest that she had never seen? It must be psychologically significant that he steals the wife of Lewis Tarrant, the most pathetic of all her dilettante characters.

Certainly there is no mystery about the appearance of Lewis Tarrant. He is in that long tradition of frigid gentlemen that stretches all the way back to the Roman spectator of her girlhood sonnet who tossed the rose to his condemned sweetheart in the arena. We understand both why Tarrant attracts and why he repels. He has every gift except the ability to make use of his gifts. His intelligence is made ineffective by his distrust of it, and his acts of kindness fail to be appreciated by the beneficiaries, who suspect the self-interest behind them. Tarrant, like most petty tyrants, is hollow inside, and Halo, his wife, is always able to collapse him with one sure thrust. Yet we are made aware of the panic behind his thin handsome front and can even feel sorry for him when Halo bears down too hard. The only false note in Tarrant's character is his desire in the end to leave Halo for Mrs. Pulsifer, and Edith must have sensed this herself, for in the sequel, *The Gods Arrive*, we see Tarrant more characteristically holding onto his wife and enjoying the torture of refusing her a divorce. A dog in the manger is what he must always be.

The hero, Vance Weston, is not only not a dilettante; he appears actually to have been conceived in terms of opposites to Lewis Tarrant. He is Midwestern, unsubtle, gauche, brutally honest, and, above all, passionately dedicated to his art. He emerges from a section of America that reveres only the present to become intoxicated by his first whiff of the past. He is sincere, openhearted, decent in his instincts; he hurts people because of his obsessive preoccupations, never by design. He is, in short, a thoroughly attractive bull in a thoroughly ridiculous china shop, and the reader is delighted to see him smash it to pieces. Weston is the breath of cleansing wind that is meant to bring fresh air to the bogus literary world of New York, with its greedy editors, its silly rich female prizegivers, and its faddy authors of current best sellers. It is unfortunate that Edith's satire of the china shop is almost as heavy as the horns and hoofs of her young bull. It makes these chapters rather noisy reading, but this is apart from the success of Weston as a character.

She has, it is true, a little difficulty in getting him started. He is almost too "hick" in the beginning. Could a young man who boasted that he had founded a new religion while in college, who rhymed "dawn" with "lorn," and whose response to a chance reference to the temple at Delphi was "The First Church of Christ at Delphi? Christian Science, you mean?" ever have turned into a serious novelist? His abruptness, too, is overdone. When Halo first haps upon him in the library of a deserted country house, he betrays no surprise at her totally unexpected presence, but simply raises the book that he is reading and demands: "Who wrote this?" Later, when he wants to learn Italian, he asks her, married woman and busy hostess though she then is: "Say, could I come round evenings, three or four times a week, and read him [Dante] with you after supper?" But these are details. The principal thing about Vance is that he is a writer. Everything and everybody are grist to his mill: the world entrances him, but he is never so seized by his trance that he does not immediately try to convert it into words. A proper name, a branch against the spring sky, an old house on the Hudson, a cocktail party, a fatuous hostess, they all have their uses to the would-be novelist. But also—and this is the darker side of the artist's character—a kiss, a family scandal, even his own marriage, have their uses for him. The essence

176

of Vance Weston is that he wants to engage passionately in the business of living, but that he can never get away from the inner eye that is always engaged in watching himself in that process and recording data to be used in a work of fiction. Nor, indeed, would he get away if he could. The artist's state of mind is like being in love; he may be unhappy, but he would not be otherwise. At the end of *Hudson River Bracketed* Vance has buried his wife and is about to start a new life with Halo Tarrant, whose husband is now willing to release her. Yet he finds that even the superior Halo, who professes such depths of understanding, requires special treatment:

> And when at last he drew her arm through his and walked beside her in the darkness to the corner where she had left her motor, he wondered if at crucial moments the same veil of unreality would always fall between himself and the soul nearest him, if the creator of imaginary things must always feel alone among the real ones.

These are the last lines of the novel, and they strike a personal note that is rare in Edith's fiction. What was the identification between the rough, passionate Middle Western boy who gets drunk after a ball game and the cultivated expatriate of the Pavillon Colombe, armed, as we glimpse her in Lubbock's book, with a pair of clippers, ready for the daily task of shearing the heads of yesterday's roses? The answer may be more obvious to those who write novels than to those who read them. Vance Weston is an extension of Edith's vision of herself, freed from the impediments of her sex, generation, and background, and, perhaps more importantly, freed from her own preoccupation with the details of decorating the physical world. Furthermore, he is intended to be a great novelist, or at least to have the makings of one. He is to be an American Tolstoi, and Edith was far too clear-sighted to have believed for a minute

177

that she would ever occupy such a role. The steps in his literary career are not the same as her own, but they are sufficiently analogous to be deeply understood: the first messy, emotional poems, the sudden strike forward with the short story molded out of the lava of a catastrophic personal experience, the more mature development of the story based on digested experience, and the first real success with the charming, nostalgic novelette about an old house and an old maid in the Hudson Valley. Now Weston feels that he is ready for the great sprawling vigorous American novel to deal with the vastness and horror and fascination of New York, but he is premature, and we feel the hopelessness of its opening chapters. He wisely abandons the book, and at the end he is about to start work on a story to be entitled "Magic." It is to deal with the epistemology of the creative process, the phenomenon of the tiny center of concentrated activity in which creatures born without their authors will live out their complicated and passionate lives.

I do not think it a coincidence, but the result of Edith's intuition of the nature of the creative process in her native land, that the year in which *Hudson River Bracketed* was published saw the appearance of a first novel by a young man who bore a marked resemblance to her hero. Thomas Wolfe was of Weston's generation and had some of Weston's explosive temperament, his roughness, his generosity, and his extreme sensitivity. Wolfe, like Weston, lived his fiction and made exhaustive, specific use of his personal experiences as subject matter for his novels. Yet the fact that he could make literary use of his love affairs did not mean that he was a cold or detached man. His life and his books were equally passionate. Wolfe was fascinated by New York, fascinated by parties and hostesses, astringently observant of all that was bogus in the literary world, easily enthusiastic and easily embittered, at once naïve and murderously shrewd. It is astonishing that a woman who had turned her face as resolutely and for as many years away from the

Thomas Wolfe.

land of her birth as Edith, should, in her late sixties, have so accurately conceived a career and personality so innately American.

So much, alas, cannot be said of her picture of life in the American Midwest which she had to work up out of Sinclair Lewis. The opening chapters of *Hudson River Bracketed* read like a parody of *Main Street* with their heavy emphasis on the crassness of small-town realtors and evangelists, and the episode when young Vance catches his grandfather in a rendezvous with his own girl friend shows Edith almost comically trying to keep apace with the sensationalism of her younger contemporaries. But happily at an early stage of Vance Weston's history she lifts him—albeit with a pair of tweezers—out of the spiritual desert of Euphoria and removes him to the Hudson River Valley, where he can contemplate an old bracketed house and read English poetry in the quiet library of a long-dead old maid. From here on, Edith is on surer ground.

There is, however, one further lapse in the novel that is too amusing not to record. We have seen that Edith was never at ease with writers who did not share her code of social restraints. She had probably never been to a literary party in New York, and she may have composed this passage to convince herself that she had missed nothing:

> "Poor old Fynes," another of them took it up, "sounded as if he'd struck a new note because he made his people talk in the vernacular. Nothing else new about *him*—might have worked up his method out of Zola. Probably did."
>
> "Zola—who's he?" somebody yawned.
>
> "Oh, I dunno. The French Thackeray, I guess."
>
> "See here, fellows, who's ready Thackeray, anyhow?"
>
> "Nobody since Lytton Strachey, I guess."
>
> "Well, anyway, *This Globe* is one great big

book. Eh, Vance, that the way you see it?"

Vance roused himself and looked at the speaker. "Not the way I see life. Life's continuous!"

"Life continuous—continuous? Why, it's a series of jumps in the dark. That's Mendel's law, anyhow," another budding critic took up the argument.

"Gee! Who's Mendel? Another new novelist?"

13

FINALE

Edith's literary and social activity continued unabated to the end. In the last seven years of her life she published four volumes of short stories, a novel, and her memoirs, and at her death she left an unfinished novel and an anthology of love poetry. But around her the old faces were disappearing. Most painful were the losses in her own household. She wrote Henriette Haven in 1933:

> My poor old Gross has failed, mentally, as well as physically, and is now a mere little harmless wraith installed at the Convent de L'Espérance here (a nursing home), and not even aware that she is no longer with me. But all this is in the order of nature and long foreseen; what prevented my going to the Berensons, as I was to do six weeks ago, was the sudden and alarming illness of my dear maid Elise, who came to me twenty years ago and inherited the household tradition of Gross. After a month's hard struggle on the part of nurses and doctors, she died three days ago of pernicious anemia, and I find myself, in my lonely old age, suddenly deprived of these two faithful affections —as well!—of all the countless stores of household experience which the two shared between them. I feel like a very old infant launched alone on the world.

Edith with Sir Stephen Runciman, William R. Tyler,
Bettine Mary Tyler, and Royall Tyler (the baby).

The most intimate friend of the last years was Elesina Tyler, an Italian who had married Royall Tyler, the American scholar and author of a biography of Charles V. She had been previously married, and the circumstances of her divorce had caused some unfavorable comment in that day of stricter rules. Edith came to know her in war work, where she had been of invaluable assistance, and she took up her cause, socially, against any who raised eyebrows. In the ensuing years the friendship deepened until, after Walter Berry's death, Mrs. Tyler was the person closest to Edith in the world. There was a good deal of criticism of this new friend by old ones, just as there had been criticism of Walter Berry. Beatrix Farrand made it clear to all that she considered Mrs. Tyler a designing person who had insinuated herself into her aunt's affections, and Edith's testamentary generosity to her friend naturally confirmed such suppositions in the minds of her kin.

It is difficult to assess such matters, but it is obvious that a considerable amount of jealousy entered into these judgments of Mrs. Tyler. I incline to think that Edith, who was a sharp judge of character, knew best what was good for her. She trusted and loved both Walter Berry and Elesina Tyler, and I see no evidence that her trust and love were misplaced.

I also suspect that Mrs. Tyler, particularly in the last lonely years, was able to give Edith the constant attention and devotion that she could get from nobody else. The other friends were inclined to find Edith possessive, and no doubt she was. Nicky Mariano says that she never quite forgave Percy Lubbock for marrying. Mrs. Chanler found that Edith was outraged when she was obliged to default on a trip because of a domestic crisis: "She [Edith] is so sure that family ties are a sort of amiable weakness that she helps one to forego them cheerfully in her excellent company—at least for a while—then they reassert themselves." But Edith's unreasonable craving for complete loyalty is more understandable when one considers that she had neither

Elesina Tyler (Mrs. Royall Tyler).

spouse nor child. Mrs. Tyler may have given her what even Walter Berry did not.

In the summer of 1937 Edith suffered a stroke from which she made only a partial recovery. Her vision was impaired and her memory affected. Mrs. Tyler and Beatrix Farrand were both with her, and a hospital routine was established. When Madame Saint-René Taillandier called, she found Edith "neat and elegant" as ever, but after a few minutes' chat in the library they were interrupted by an obviously anxious attendant. The rest of the visit was spent in the garden:

> A servant pushed her wheel-chair, and she set forth to examine her roses, carefully and seriously as in other days; we followed three paces behind, that she might not exert herself to talk. Silently she held out a rose to me; I took it and kept it, knowing it to be the last good-bye; a wave of the hand, and I left her.

Beatrix Farrand was sufficiently encouraged by her aunt's condition to return to the United States. She wrote to Gaillard Lapsley: "Mrs. Tyler and her family and White are those who she wants near her, and while she is glad to see the rest of us, without doubt, we also are fading and our absences not noticed as they formerly would have been."

Edith died while Beatrix Farrand was at sea. The latter wrote again to Lapsley upon landing:

> We have lost an incomparable friend. We shall find it an empty, queer world without her, and already one feels the void where one could ever before rely on her wisdom, keenness, appreciation and justice. What an example she is of a beautiful construction built around a great gift.

Robert Norton described the funeral service to Lapsley:

186

Beatrix Jones Farrand (Mrs. Max Farrand), the only grandchild of Edith's parents.

I went up from here for the funeral, at which most of her intimates were present, though not John [John Hugh-Smith], who could not get back from Italy in time nor B. B. [Bernard Berenson]. Kenneth Clark came over and Johnny Johnston travelled up with me. There were twenty or thirty in all, I suppose, counting the household. The cemetery is the only unrepellent one I know near Paris. The forest trees come down the slope among the graves and there are perhaps fewer monumental horrors than in most French churchyards. The prayers were said at the graveside and then the friends, who included poor old Walter Gay, slowly dispersed. Poor old White was gravely composed—his life work ended. I imagine she will have left him well provided for but I have heard nothing of the will.

The will, or wills (there was a French as well as an American one) came as a bit of a shock to some of the friends, for Elesina Tyler received the bulk of Edith's property. There was even a legal question as to whether the trust under Edith's mother's will passed to Beatrix Farrand as the sole heir of the Joneses or to Mrs. Tyler as Edith's residuary legatee. The two ladies litigated the matter and ultimately settled it, but, needless to say, it did not improve their relations.

The intensification of interest in American history and letters in the past twenty years has assured a permanent place for the fiction of Edith Wharton. She has become required reading for students who want a picture of Eastern-seaboard upper-class living of the turn of the century. The very aspect of her writing that has put off so many readers—her concern with rich and cultivated Americans, usually New Yorkers, who did not have to earn their living—ironically enough, has contributed to her enduring fame.

It may seem unfair that so many people should have criticized her for writing about what she knew best, but the fault in these matters usually lies with the author. Tolstoi confined *War and Peace* to a handful of aristocratic characters without being called a snob because he saw mankind in every man. Edith did not see quite all this behind her characters. It is difficult to detach them from the settings to which they are so precisely fastened. Her imagination did not reach out to the "great unwashed"; its scope was limited to what she recognized as her peculiar province. This is true of most writers. There are very few Tolstois. But it keeps Edith out of the tiny class of the greatest novelists. Even in so superb a tale as *Ethan Frome*, where the characters are humble folk, one has a sense of the *tour de force* of the skilled craftsman. But what of this? It is better to be grateful for the illuminating intelligence that permeates her work.

With the posthumously published books, *The Buccaneers* and *Ghosts*, her fiction totals to thirty-two volumes. Probably her ultimate reputation in American letters will rest upon a small fraction of this list: *Ethan Frome, The House of Mirth, The Custom of the Country, The Age of Innocence, Old New York*, and a few short stories: "Pomegranate Seed," "Roman Fever," "After Holbein." Many other writers have attempted to delineate the New York society of old brownstone and new wealth, but the reason that she succeeded where almost all of them failed is that, in addition to her great gifts as an artist, her lucidity, her wit, her style, she had a tight grasp of just what this society was made up of. She understood that it was arbitrary, capricious, and inconsistent; she was aware that it did not hesitate to abolish its standards while most loudly proclaiming them. She knew when money could open doors and when it couldn't, when lineage would serve and when it would be merely sneered at. She knew that compromises could be counted on, but that they were rarely made while still considered compromises. She knew her men and women of property, recently or anciently acquired, how they decorated their houses and

where they spent their summers. She realized, in short, that the social game was played without rules, and this made her one of the few novelists before Proust who could describe it with profundity.

If anyone says that what she did was not worth doing, I can only answer that the society of which she wrote was an integral part of the American dream—the American myth—the American illusion.

The grave. The inscription "O Crux Ave Spes Unica" was chosen by Edith and aroused speculation among her friends that she may have had more religious feeling than she ever demonstrated.